Find Your F*cking Fire

Poems on Embracing Anger for Social Change

Anne Kinsey

TENOM
CENTER

Tehom Center Publishing is a 501(c)3 nonprofit publishing feminist and queer authors, with a commitment to elevate BIPOC writers. Its face and voice is Rev. Dr. Angela Yarber.

Paperback ISBN: 978-1-966655-52-7

Ebook ISBN: 978-1-966655-53-4

Contents

To our younger selves, whose anger and fire are sacred.

"Our anger arises over our pain and is only pointing back to our pain. To hold space for our pain is a way that we begin to take care of our pain."

— LAMA ROD OWENS, *LOVE AND RAGE*

Introduction

When Donald J. Trump took office for the second time on January 20th, 2025, my family's life immediately descended into chaos.

Anti-trans executive orders impacted my teen's passport, and we spent weeks scrambling to get their documents back. With the help of lawyers, a few nonprofits, and a senator's office, we finally did, but not before wondering whether we might need to figure out how to flee the country without their documents.

At the same time, anti-DEI executive orders gutted work contracts and slashed my income during a time when we were already living in poverty. Weekly food pantry trips, stretching meals with food stamps, and relying on Medicaid to manage chronic conditions punctuated our days. Then came the day our utilities were shut off. Mutual aid from friends and family got the lights back on and helped with other unmet needs.

My son had a traumatic visit with a fatphobic medical provider. I was filing complaints with the state medical board and, separately, chasing down overdue payments from an anti-trafficking organization that had not paid me for my labor. During a leisurely walk in downtown Blowing Rock, North Carolina, a hiking boot malfunction sent me flying onto the pavement. I sprained both elbows, cracked ribs, and scraped up my body, leaving me so injured that I needed help just to shower.

All of this happened alongside everything else unfolding in our lives, with my oldest graduating from high school and preparing for university, my middle child moving up from middle school, and my youngest dreaming about opening a gluten-free bakery someday. I was also releasing my first book, *Mosaic Hearts*, attending signings, and celebrating the launches of dear friends' books.

Through it all, significant grief lingered and compounded as we witnessed brutal ICE crackdowns, the return of what amounts to concentration camps on United States soil, the dismantling of government agencies, massive job losses, and the passage of Trump's One Big Beautiful Bill. Our financial survival was already hanging by a thread. Now, we were witnessing a country that had always been violent for many of us become even more dangerous and dystopian with each passing day.

I knew I was hurting, but I had not yet realized that to feel so much pain was to carry just as much anger. Hurt is part of the anger family. While I had been naming my feelings, saying things like, "I am furious about ICE, racism, and transphobia," I was not letting myself fully feel them. I was bypassing my anger in the name of survival, overfunctioning my way through emergency exit plans, advocacy, freelance gigs, and PhD applications. In all of my busyiness, I had not stopped to ask myself where my fire had gone.

Most of us are taught to suppress our anger. School, family, media, government, and society teach us to smile through injustice, thank people for crumbs, and swallow our rage. Suppression is how empire protects itself. It keeps us palatable, quiet, and easily controlled, then convinces us we are neither worthy of nor safe enough to demand equity.

Several weeks ago, I found myself teetering on the edge of burnout. In therapy, I described it somatically. I felt a heavy knot in my gut, tightness in my throat, and a bone-deep exhaustion that went far beyond fatigue. I began to voice what I was feeling and found myself literally roaring.

During that session, I brought up a practice a medical qigong doctor had once taught me. I visualized an opening in the earth where I could release my anger, grief, and burdens. I roared into the void and felt the beginning of relief.

By the next session, I felt more energetic, but when I tried to release more anger, something caught. In my solar plexus, I felt a sticky knot. It was cool, tight, thorned, and vibrating with resistance. I tried to pull it out, but it clung to me like it did not want to let go.

As a Sagittarius, I am used to feeling fire there. I usually sense a swirling, twirling, energizing flame. This felt like a dead zone. No wonder I was so depleted.

My therapist helped me see what I had been unaware of. In my effort to survive, I had been storing my anger instead of processing it. I was using gratitude to avoid sitting with my fury, and it was making me sick.

In trying to care for everyone else, I had lost my connection to the fire inside me. Without that fire, how could I possibly fight for a better world?

The next day, I had a massage with my friend Trish. I told her about the energy blockage in my solar plexus and she placed a singing bowl over it. The vibrations moved through me, shaking something loose.

Trish suggested that perhaps my fire had not gone out, but rather had burned so intensely it turned to lava and hardened over. She encouraged me to imagine that hardened lava breaking free and releasing through my body. Something clicked. My anger wanted to move through my fingertips and onto the page.

That same day, the idea for this book was born. Within twenty-four hours, I sent the outline and thesis to my publisher. She gave me the green light, and I wrote the entire book in less than a month.

Writing is one of the ways I reconnect with my anger and transform it into something powerful. When I write books, share posts, or organize for change, my anger becomes a force for connection, community, and equity. As such, this book poured out of me like a sacred partnership with the Universe. It is both a personal anger toolkit and a collective offering for anyone who has ever asked where their fire went. I wrote this book because I believe we will not get free without our anger. We cannot make the world safer or more just if we do not learn to listen to our rage, embrace it, and let it lead us toward change.

Find Your Fucking Fire: Poems on Embracing Anger for Social Change invites you to make friends with your anger in ways that transform your life and the world around you. Together, we will explore how and why we were taught to suppress anger, how to excavate it from our bodies, embrace its many forms, express and release it, and harness its power for the collective good. Through a mix of memoir-infused, psychoeducational, and reflective poetry, personal reflections, and writing prompts, we will reclaim anger as a force for healing, empowerment, and revolution.

Let's find your fucking fire.

SUPPRESS

How and Why We Were Taught to Suppress Our Anger

"The most common way people give up their power
is by thinking they don't have any."

— ALICE WALKER

Ponderings on Anger Suppression

Soraya Chemaly famously said, "Anger is an assertion of rights and worth,"[1] and this is precisely why so many of us are socialized to suppress it. From the moment we are old enough to cry with frustration, we are often told to quiet down, calm down, or settle down. We are told to stop crying, be polite, and smile even when we feel like we are coming undone. Over time, these messages begin to stick, and we learn that anger is something shameful, dangerous, inappropriate, or a sign that something is wrong with us. We begin to hold our tongues and suppress our feelings to survive, especially if we hold multiple historically marginalized identities and live in realities where we are already under scrutiny.

By the time we reach adulthood, we have learned to perform composure at the expense of our inner truth. Often, we do not even recognize our anger when it shows up. Instead, we feel a vague sense of unease or discomfort. It might manifest as exhaustion, bitterness, or helplessness. We may notice physical tension, emotional overwhelm, or chronic stress. We feel the effects of anger even when we have been trained not to name it as such. That confusion is also part of our internalized suppression.

This section explores how and why we were taught to suppress our anger, not just on a personal level, but also through collective and systemic conditioning. When anger is labeled as dangerous, deviant, or uncivil, oppressive systems remain unchallenged. When people fear their own anger, they are less likely to ask questions, demand justice, or insist on change.

Many strategies are used to teach us that anger is not allowed. Some are overt, such as punishment, shaming, or public humiliation. Others are more insidious, like tone policing, labeling anger as a mental health issue, or pathologizing it through oppressive spiritual frameworks. We see these messages in families that avoid conflict, in media that portrays marginalized people as unstable or violent, in classrooms that

---

1. Soraya Chemaly, *Rage Becomes Her: The Power of Women's Anger* (New York: Atria Books, 2018)

15

reward quiet compliance, and in workplaces that equate "professionalism" with silence.

Our institutions are built to condition us. Schools teach us to sit still and follow rules. Workplaces train us to remain polite no matter how unjust the situation is. Religious institutions teach that anger is sinful or spiritually immature. Gender roles and the gender binary reinforce the idea that only certain people are allowed to express anger, and even then, only in narrow, socially sanctioned ways. Racism adds another layer. Anger expressed by Black people, for example, is far more likely to be labeled threatening or violent than the same emotion expressed by white people. These layered forms of oppression shape not only who is granted space for anger, but also how that anger is interpreted, received, and punished.

For many of us, especially those who are queer, trans, fat, disabled, neurodivergent, racialized, or otherwise marginalized, the consequences of expressing anger can be severe. We are told our anger is irrational, accused of being aggressive, and blamed for the very harm we are reacting to. We are gaslit, silenced, and punished. Sometimes this happens in personal relationships. Other times it leads to job loss, institutionalization, incarceration, or violence. For those of us who have experienced human trafficking, abuse, or systemic trauma, anger may have felt so dangerous to express that we learned to disconnect from it entirely.

Even given all of this, anger is not the enemy. It is a messenger. Anger tells us when our boundaries have been crossed. It signals that something is unjust, unfair, or out of alignment. It rises in defense of dignity, life, and love. As Chemaly reminds us, it is an assertion of worth. It says, "I matter, my people matter, our pain matters, and what is happening is not okay." This is why anger is so heavily policed. When people begin to trust their anger, they start telling the truth. They stop apologizing. They stop complying. Instead, they begin to organize, resist, and demand something better. Anger disrupts systems that rely on our silence.

Suppressing our anger does not make it disappear. It makes it fester. It settles into our bodies, leaks out sideways, poisons our sense of self, and wears us down. Over time, suppressed anger contributes to illness, mental health challenges, and a deep disconnection from our own inner compass.

To reclaim our anger, we must first understand how it was taken from us. We must name the tactics and systems that taught us to suppress it. When we examine these patterns in the open, we can begin the work of healing the split between what we feel and what we have been allowed to express.

This section gathers the many ways anger has been stolen from us and names the forces behind that theft. It is not exhaustive. If you think of other ways your anger has been suppressed, I invite you to add your voice to the chorus. Together, we will point to the roots of suppression and challenge the messages that told us our anger made us unworthy, dangerous, or unlovable. As you move through these pages, notice where these patterns show up in your own life. Notice where your anger grew quiet and what was happening at the time. Let yourself grieve what you were not allowed to feel. Let yourself remember.

Your anger was never the problem. Suppressing it was.

How Anger is Suppressed

"I have lived with that anger, ignoring it, feeding upon it, learning to use it before it laid my visions to waste, for most of my life. Once I did it in silence, afraid of the weight. My fear of anger taught me nothing. Your fear of that anger will teach you nothing, also."

— AUDRE LORDE, *THE USES OF ANGER*

Ponderings on How Anger is Suppressed

Many of us were not taught to understand anger. Instead, we were taught to fear it, suppress it, and eventually forget we ever had it. Reclaiming our anger begins with recognizing the quiet, persistent ways it was stripped from us, until those messages shaped our sense of self.

We are told that anger is immature, unproductive, irrational, shameful, unspiritual, gendered, threatening, or even dangerous. We are urged to be "the bigger person," to "let it go," to "rise above," and to "keep the peace." These ideas are embedded in the fabric of our lives and woven through family dynamics, school rules, religious teachings, media portrayals, and workplace norms. We hear them in sermons and therapy sessions, during performance reviews, in friendships, and at the dinner table. Over time, these messages become so normalized that we often fail to notice we have internalized them.

Sometimes, we come to believe we no longer feel anger at all. We might even take pride in this. We imagine that being above anger is a sign of emotional maturity or spiritual growth, even though it is often just evidence of suppression. I know this because I have lived it.

There was a time when I believed I was no longer an angry person, and that I had overcome anger such that it rarely visited me. As a teen who had once been prone to angry outbursts, this felt like progress. The way I expressed anger in the past had sometimes caused harm to myself and others, so I thought the absence of anger meant I was healed.

What I did not recognize was that eliminating anger was not the goal. The true aim is to feel our anger and express it in ways that are empowering, honest, and aligned with our values. Eventually, I began to understand that the absence of anger was not a sign of healing. It was a symptom of disconnection. Something deep within me had been silenced.

Anger, when expressed with intention and awareness, is not destructive. It brings clarity, protection, and direction. It helps us name harm, draw boundaries, and know when something must change for us to feel safe.

When anger is suppressed, we may feel numb, flat, overly anxious, or falsely cheerful. We might become consumed with people-pleasing or conflict avoidance. Our bodies may carry the weight of suppression through tension, fatigue, mental fog, or dissociation. We might say "I'm fine" when we are not. We may cry when we are actually furious. We might spiral into shame, guilt, or self-blame instead of naming harm. When anger is unwelcome in the systems around us, it often becomes unwelcome within us.

The poems in this section explore the many ways we are taught to suppress our anger. This list is not exhaustive. You are welcome to reflect, write, or add your own experiences with anger suppression as part of this truth-telling work. As you do, you might begin to recognize the patterns named in the following poems, as well as how they have shaped your own life.

Some of the messages described in this section are blatant and aggressive, including punishment, ridicule, rejection, or violence. Others are more covert, such as gaslighting, conflict avoidance, spiritual bypassing, tone policing, or rewards for silence and self-sacrifice. These poems hold up a mirror to the cultural, familial, religious, educational, and political conditioning that has taught us to disconnect from our anger. Some may feel validating. Others might feel tender or even triggering. Be gentle with yourself as you read. Honor your emotional state and trauma history. Take breaks if you need them. Return when you are ready, with the support you need.

This is not easy work. Noticing how much anger you have held inside, or how long you have lived without recognizing it, can stir discomfort, confusion, or grief. These are not signs of failure. They are signs that something important is surfacing for care. Rather than rushing through, stay curious. Let yourself feel what arises without judgment. Move through this section in whatever way best supports your healing.

Your anger matters. Your truth matters. You matter.

Shaming Messages

You are too much.
Calm down.
Go to your room.

What's with
your attitude?
Why are you
so angry?

I should record you,
so you can see
how you look
when you scream.

What would
they think?
After all I've
done for you.

Don't be
so sensitive.
I was only
kidding.

Be a lady.
Watch your
tone.

Don't cause
a scene.
What will the
neighbors think?

Why do you always
make it about ____?

No need to play
the ____ card.

You are difficult,
manipulative,
unforgiving, sinful,
unreasonable, faithless,
problematic,
crazy, divisive,
out of your
fucking mind,
and I want
nothing to do
with you.

You should be
ashamed
of yourself.

Tone Policing

Good oppressed people
know you get more flies
with honey than vinegar.

Speak calmly,
politely, kindly,
sweetly smiling,
apologetically fawning
your colonizer,
oppressor, abuser,
user, family, friends.

You wouldn't want to
hurt their feelings.

You make a good point,
but I don't like
how you say it.
Code switch.

Watch your attitude.
Assume the best.
I can't hear you
like this.

Don't take that tone
with me, young lady.

Be diplomatic,
respectful, kind.
Don't confront.
Use "I statements."

Don't emote,
stay positive,

not so harsh,
think about others,
and if you can't say
something nice,
don't say
anything at all.

Education

Disruptive behavior
means detention,
suspension,
expulsion,
permanently marked.
So, do not argue.

Obedience
means gold stars.
Silence and politeness
equal praise, love,
and recognition.

Respect
your authorities.
Follow the rules,
dress codes,
speech codes,
tone codes,
conduct codes.

Compliance,
deference, and
cishet-centered
white praise
for racialized,
disabled, neurodiverse,
fat, trans, queer,
othered students.

Regulate
your emotions
into compliance.
Leave aggressive
(passionate)

responses
at the door.

Everyone here
helps you grow up,
mature, move past
your failures
of self-expression,
find neutrality,
objectivity, and
override contrary
tendencies or protest.

Emotional labor
with a smile.
Take abuse
without reaction.
Receive punishment
while disbelieved,
and thank us.

Apologize now.

Ignore history
when others might
be offended
by the horror
of what was
and still is,
their "innocent"
intentions exposed
as evil.

Gender

Be a lady.
Be nice.
It's hormones.
You are so
irrational.
Don't raise
your voice.
Such a
fucking
BITCH!
Bossy, bitter,
crazy,
hysterical.
Slut!
Dramatic,
acting out.
He didn't
mean it.
Defer to
men always.
Obey
with a smile.

Man up.
Get over it.
Control yourself.
Take charge.
Never ever
show weakness.
Don't be
such a pussy.
Suck it up.
Only bitches
act like that.
Don't be a baby.

Never ever
let them get to you.
Don't let them
see you sweat.
Don't make
a big deal.
Be a Transformer,
GI Joe, show them
what you've got.
Macho robot.

Stop fussing.
You just want
to be weird.
So confused.
Be normal,
pick a gender,
and stop whining.
Don't be
difficult.
Stop centering
your identity.
This is why
people hate
trans people.
You are hurting
the movement,
so tone it down,
let it go,
not so sensitive.
Stop bringing
it up, you fuck-up.
Disappear.

Toxic Christianity

Anger is sin,
and so are you.

Your thoughts
dictate your
emotions, so
think on everything
true, honorable,
just, pure, lovely,
commendable,
excellent, and
worthy of praise.
It honors God
to bypass it.

With every
angry thought,
scream inside:
IN THE NAME
OF JESUS,
SATAN GET
BEHIND ME!
Take your thoughts
captive. Have faith.

A gentle answer
turns away wrath.
Be slow to anger.
Put away all
bitterness.
Submit to
authority.
Anger separates
you from God,
so stop it.

Die to yourself.
Don't be divisive.
Jesus would be
so ashamed of you.

What if God
saw you now?
Become more
spiritually mature.
Have an exorcism.
Confess your sins.
Stop the witchcraft.
Repent now.

Good Christians
never say that.
You're giving Satan
a foothold.
Rebellion is sin.
Pray about it.
Don't complain.
I'll pray for you.

God wants peace
for you, so search
your heart for
unforgiveness
and ask forgiveness.

Do not conform
to the patterns
of this world.
Meditate on
God's truth,
HIS perfect
will for you,
and love one
another without

anger. Do you
know that you know
that you know
where you are
going when you die?

Polite Society

We don't get political.
Stay rational, calm,
cool and collected.

Leave your anger
at home, not here.

Stay objective.
Find a better way
to say that.

You are making
us uncomfortable.
Do not alienate
anyone, and be civil.

Check your emotions
at the door. Reactivity
isn't welcome here.

We all have struggles,
so don't blow this
out of proportion.

Calm and neutral
discourse always
achieves the best
results.

Isn't that what you want?

Consequences

Your anger
deserves
punishment.

Labels:
disruptive,
defiant,
unprofessional,
uncooperative,
unstable,
crazy,
too emotional,
problematic.

Consequences:
isolation,
negative remarks,
public shaming,
ridicule,
abandonment,
shunning,
silent treatment,
name calling,
calling out.

No recess,
field trips,
leadership roles,
promotions,
love, or
relationships.

Physical:
restraint,
slapping,

beating,
teaching you
a lesson.

Write-ups,
performance plans,
improvement plans,
conflict resolution,
groundings,
privileges lost,
forced apologies,
lost income,
social isolation,
disbelief.

Comfort others with
anger locked away.

Gaslighting

You're overreacting
and making things up.
It wasn't like that,
and she means well.

You are always
so fucking sensitive,
looking for something
to cause a ruckus about,
making it about you.

That was so long ago.
Why bring it up now?

Making mountains
out of molehills.
I never said that.
Nobody else
is causing a stink.

You're acting crazy,
creating problems,
just being negative,
begging for attention,
playing the victim,
blowing things
way out of proportion.

It's not that serious.
I wouldn't have done it
if you hadn't done that.

I love you, despite you
provoking me,

clearly on purpose.
Just look at your
behavior.
Wow.

Reflective Pause: Gaslighting

Gaslighting is a powerful tool of control and manipulation. It distorts a person's sense of reality and erodes their trust in their own emotions, memories, and perceptions. In this poem, the repetition of common gaslighting phrases becomes a chorus of silencing, delegitimizing, and minimizing. For many of us who have endured emotional abuse, systemic oppression, or both, this language is painfully familiar. These statements may seem mundane or harmless to outsiders, but for survivors, they accumulate like stones, forming walls of confusion, shame, and self-doubt.

In my work with survivors of human trafficking and systemic violence, I often hear stories of gaslighting, both by abusers and by the very systems meant to offer support. Survivors are told they are lying, over-reacting, or mentally unwell. They are punished for advocating for themselves or expressing emotional responses to harm. When anger naturally arises from these experiences, it is often twisted and used as further evidence that the person is irrational, unstable, or dangerous. This cycle isolates people and reinforces harmful narratives, all while protecting those who caused the harm.

Recognizing these patterns is a vital step in reclaiming power and reconnecting with the truth of our lived experiences.

Reflective Writing

Take a moment to reflect on a time when your anger or emotional pain was minimized, dismissed, or labeled as irrational. What phrases were used? What impact did they have on your sense of self? How did you respond in the moment, and how do you wish you had been able to respond?

If it feels safe enough, try writing a response to those gaslighting messages. Speak back. Name the truth. Let your anger move through the page without censoring or editing it. If it helps, begin with: "That was not the truth. The truth is…"

Let your words be raw and unfiltered. Give voice to what you know deep down. Let that truth rise and breathe freely on the page, maybe even for the first time ever.

Pathologized

It's trauma.
Just calm down.
Regulate your
nervous system.

You need help,
a therapist.
Take your meds,
you're clearly
out of your mind.

You're manic,
spiraling out
of control.
BPD for sure,
scaring people.

You're triggered
and don't *really*
feel this way.
Take deep breaths.
You'll see.

You're delusional,
having a breakdown.
Unhealthy behavior,
completely paranoid.
Time for the hospital.

Praise

Such a good student,
mature for your age.

Thank you for
not making a fuss.

I wish everyone
handled things like you.

You're the calm one,
always dependable.

So professional,
composed and quiet.

So reasonable,
neat and contained.

Team player,
never overreacts.

Graceful under pressure,
rising above.

Not the angry type,
handles things with tact.

Evolved, grounded,
peaceful energy.

Always the high road,
always putting others first.

Bias

So aggressive.
No need to be hostile.
Calm down,
nobody is attacking you.
You are scaring people,
intimidating the group.
They will think you are
one of *those*
Black people.

You are militant,
radical, too political
for this space.
Be more peaceful,
like Gandhi.
They will think
you are like 9/11.
Where are you from again?

You are picking fights,
being divisive.
You are why people
do not support queer
and trans folx.
Too much identity,
pushing people away.

My daughter is autistic,
so I know this is not
a meltdown.
You are manipulating.
Irrational, toxic,
too sensitive,
overreacting.
Work on your

emotional control.

Uneducated,
no work ethic.
Jealous of success,
stuck in poverty.
Be grateful
for what you have.
Stay positive,
it attracts success.

You are a problem patient,
attention-seeking.
Damn lucky
we are helping you.
Do not bite the hand
that feeds you.
You make it harder
for other disabled people.

Too fat,
lacks self-control.
It is mental illness,
your rage,
your body.
I am only concerned
for your health.
You should thank me
for helping you.

Reflective Pause: Bias

Anger perceptions are inequitable when some bodies are given the benefit of the doubt, while others are instantly labeled dangerous, irrational, or unstable. This poem offers a striking window into the biases and assumptions often embedded in how anger is perceived and policed. Statements directed at the speaker reveal attempts to silence anger while also pathologizing, stereotyping, and dehumanizing the person expressing it. These reactions are laced with racism, fatphobia, ableism, queerphobia, xenophobia, classism, and more. In many communities, and especially for people who live with intersectionality, anger is seen as a threat rather than a valid form of expression.

Through my work supporting survivors of human trafficking and other trauma, I have seen how often this kind of bias surfaces in systems that are meant to offer care. Survivors are labeled as manipulative, noncompliant, aggressive, or mentally unwell simply for speaking up or having valid emotional responses. These narratives are weaponized to withhold support, discredit lived experience, and maintain control. The result is further trauma, along with an internalized message that one must be small, agreeable, and silent to be seen as worthy of help. Recognizing these patterns allows us to challenge them and support one another in reclaiming anger as a sign of humanity rather than pathology.

Reflective Writing

Have you ever been told your anger made you scary, ungrateful, irrational, or undeserving of support? What was the identity-based message beneath that reaction? Take a few moments to explore a time when your anger was filtered through someone else's bias or stereotype.

If it feels safe enough, write a letter to yourself or to the version of you who was silenced in that moment. What do you want them to know now? How can you affirm their truth and name what was unjust? Give yourself permission to let your anger be fully seen on the page as a righteous and necessary voice that deserves to be heard.

Family Rules

We are family,
so we don't fight.

Stop making us look bad,
and be the bigger person.

Just say sorry
and don't rock the boat.

Keep the peace
and don't start drama.

Don't tell them
what I told you.

Let it go because
it's in the past.

That's just how they are,
so no point in arguing.

It's Christmas! Come on!
Let everyone have a nice time.

You are making a big deal
out of nothing.

We don't talk about that
around the kids.

You're too sensitive
and we're only kidding.

Lighten up.

Toxic Positivity

Good vibes only.
Focus on the positive.
What you focus on grows.
Everything happens
for a reason.
Let it go because
anger doesn't serve you.
Choose joy and
don't give energy
to negativity.
Look on the bright side.
It could have been worse.
Forgiveness is necessary
or you won't heal.
Happiness is a choice,
so don't let them
steal your peace.
This is just a test,
so think high-vibe thoughts.
You're too blessed
to ever be stressed.
Smile through the pain.
Gratitude fixes everything,
and like attracts like,
so your anger is
causing this.
Let your love
be louder than
your rage.

Why Anger is Suppressed

"Anger is loaded with information and energy. It is a powerful tool for survival and for change."

— AUDRE LORDE, *THE USES OF ANGER*

Ponderings on Why Anger is Suppressed

If anger connects us to our sense of worth, rights, and need for change, then it makes sense that oppressive systems would do everything possible to keep us from it. Anger is a powerful spark that leads us to recognize injustice, imagine something better, and begin to move toward it. For those who benefit from the status quo, that spark is dangerous. If enough people reclaim their anger, the systems that privilege them start to lose their grip.

Anger threatens the imposed order of systems built on hierarchy, control, and domination. White supremacy, capitalism, patriarchy, ableism, fatphobia, transphobia, and other systems of oppression depend on a population that doubts its own worth and remains afraid to speak up. Anger disrupts that by pointing directly at what hurts and demanding something better.

Anger suppression is a tool of social control. When people are taught to disconnect from their anger, they are less likely to resist injustice, form coalitions, and imagine liberatory futures. If you can keep someone questioning their right to be angry, you can often keep them from organizing, protesting, striking, creating, or even dreaming.

This is why so many forms of anger are pathologized, especially in marginalized communities. Anger in white men may be seen as strong or assertive. That same anger in Black, Indigenous, or Brown people is often labeled dangerous, unstable, or violent. A disabled person's frustration may be dismissed as emotional instability. A fat person's outrage might be written off as bitterness. A trans person's righteous anger is projected as threat or confusion. When bias shapes how anger is interpreted, it becomes easier for institutions to punish it and harder for individuals to trust it.

This punishment can be subtle or severe. It can look like exclusion from social circles or loss of job opportunities. It can look like misdiagnosis, criminalization, medical neglect, or physical violence. Over time, these consequences train us to silence ourselves before anyone else has the chance to. The fear becomes internalized, and the silence becomes reflexive.

Religious, educational, and corporate systems all play a role in rein-forcing this. Schools reward quiet compliance. Workplaces value professionalism over honesty. Religious communities preach forgive-ness before justice, spiritualizing submission and turning righteous anger into something shameful. These institutions reinforce the idea that anger is not only inappropriate, but morally wrong.

At the heart of anger suppression lies a fundamental truth. If people truly felt the full weight of their anger, many would refuse to keep living the way they have been told to. They would push back, walk away, grieve, organize, and create. They would remember their power.

This is why reclaiming our anger is a political and spiritual act. Doing so reconnects us to the parts of ourselves that know we deserve more. It offers clarity, helping us see past the lies we have been fed about our place in the world. As we do this work together, we draw closer to one another and begin building the conditions for real transformation.

The poems in this section explore the deeper logic of anger suppres-sion. They name the systems that depend on it and the fears that keep it in place. They ask us to imagine what might happen if those fears were no longer in charge. As you read, I invite you to reflect not only on what has kept your anger buried, but also on what becomes possible when it is finally allowed to rise.

Social Control

We must never threaten
the status quo,
expose injustice,
question authority,
or demand change.

We must never unite
in solidarity of purpose,
collective action,
or resistance,
reclaiming voice,
body, and truth.

We must never deconstruct
hierarchies, empire,
privilege, oppression,
assimilation, dehumanization,
colonization, exploitation,
money, or profit.

We must never activate
movements, make it harder
to control or pacify,
silence or destroy
with contagious uprising
and truth.

We must never humanize
anyone not in power,
anyone in pain,
or make the evil
fuckers uncomfortable.

Reputations

Anger threatens
curated reputations,
names harm directly,
calls in consequences,

while exposing
abusers, corruption,
hypocrisy, and
every fucked-up
system of control.

Anger refuses
to be reined in
by scripted
narratives
protecting hierarchy,

while revealing
complicity,
evil intent,
false gratitude,
and polite dissent.

Anger crushes
images, PR
campaigns,
spreads like
a roaring wildfire,

while demanding
repair without
performative bullshit.
It interrupts
gaslit falsities.

Anger resists
spiritualized silence,
never pacified by
unity, grace, or
God cards,

while rejecting
premature reconciliation
before reparations
and real change.

Anger insists
on communal clarity,
makes bigots
squirm anxiously
in discomfort,

while fueling
action through marching,
policy, whistleblowing,
or burning the
whole damn thing
down to the ground.

Anger illuminates
patterns of exploitation,
control, and systems of evil
in neon lights,

while showing
how manipulation
works to pacify
the masses,
instead of reckoning
with hard truths.

Reflective Pause: Reputations

Anger is often cast as the villain in social and political discourse, but what if it is actually the truth-teller? "Reputations" names how anger is both justified and deeply necessary. Anger challenges curated reputations, exposes harm, and resists the pacifying scripts that uphold power. When we witness injustice and feel pressure to stay calm or silent, anger rises as a subversive declaration that harm matters and that those responsible must answer for it.

Over the years, I have repeatedly witnessed institutions silence survivors' rightful rage by cloaking harm in politeness, spiritual platitudes, or so-called neutrality. These tactics do not support healing or justice. They protect systems and abusers from accountability while shifting the weight of composure onto those who have already been harmed. Anger, especially when shared in community, can be a powerful tool for revealing truth, dismantling gaslighting, and making space for real transformation. It makes those who benefit from the status quo uncomfortable, and that discomfort is often where change begins.

Reflective Writing

Think back to a time when your anger revealed a truth that others wanted to ignore. Were you pressured to stay quiet to protect someone's reputation, maintain a sense of unity, or preserve an institution's image? What did that suppression cost you?

Write a response where you let that truth have space. Say the thing no one wanted said. Name the harm and what accountability would have looked like. Allow yourself to release harmful expectations and stand firmly in the clarity your anger brings.

Uprising

Anger clarifies
shared injustice
with open eyes,

empowers people,
unites our purpose
to birth dreams again,
to fight for futures

with urgency,
blessing diversity,
disrupting isolation
with community,
as individualism
falls away.

Anger awakens
the passive to power,
sparks urgency

to explosively expose
system sewage,
fueling courage,
making refusal possible,

as masses awaken
memory and energy,
building direct action,
connecting generations
while propaganda burns,
people returning home
to one another again.

Order

Anger disrupts
politeness,
obedience,
hierarchy,
rejects meritocracy,
conditional inclusion,
binaries like
good / bad,
white / Black,
male / female,
right / wrong,
refuses silence
in the face of harm.

Anger shatters
neutrality, revealing
bloody hands
for all to see,
fractures internalized
oppression, guilt,
and shame,
until we are
big enough
to disobey
without permission,
to end
generational harm
now.

Anger calls out
false unity,
unmasks betrayal,
threatens objectivity
with lived experience,
knowledge shifting

into contagious
liberation—
and that
is what
they fear most.

Reflective Pause: Order

Anger is not the problem. Oppressive systems thrive on silence, obedience, and the illusion of peace, and this poem shows us how anger acts as a wedge between us and the expectations that keep us small. When we get angry, we often begin to see how those expectations were designed to maintain hierarchy and oppressive order. We start to question binary thinking, conditional acceptance, and all the ways we were taught to stay in line. In this way, anger becomes an invitation to unlearn and break cycles of harm.

There is immense power in naming what has kept us quiet. Anger can reveal hidden things within us and in the world around us. It loosens the grip of internalized oppression and allows us to imagine something freer. That freedom is threatening to systems invested in control, so they teach us that anger is dangerous. Still, our anger is often a sign that we are waking up, ready to disobey unjust norms, as well as create new ones that honor our full humanity.

Reflective Writing

Can you recall a moment when your anger clashed with expectations of politeness, obedience, or conformity? What were you being asked to accept or ignore? Who benefited from your silence?

Write a reflection that explores how your anger challenged those expectations. What shifted when you allowed yourself to question or resist? How might your anger be guiding you toward deeper liberation and collective change?

Status Quo

Suppressed anger
busies people with
emotional management,
appearances of harmony,
civility, conflict avoidance,
and upholding traditions,

so they don't disrupt,
seek justice, tear down
unjust systems,
or dare ask why.

Suppressed anger
ensures compliance,
fear, discouragement,
comfort, tone policing,
and bold-faced lies,

so they don't express
discontent with
dominant groups,
or say anything
of substance
to illuminate the charade.

Suppressed anger
reframes injustice
as personal grievance,
isolating people
in toxic shame,

so they don't
call it out,
truth-tell,
confront unjust

inherited power.

Suppressed anger
protects wealth
and property,
white comfort
and fragility,

so they don't
see the farce
for what it is
and decide to
blow it all
to the ground.

Productivity

Anger threatens
hierarchy, labeled
insubordination,

while labor control
prevents unions,
preserves productivity,
public image,
and legal safety,

avoids accountability
and collective action,
ensures upward
emotional labor,
rewards obedience,
punishes disruption.

Compliance is incentivized
while white, cishet,
able-bodied norms
pathologize
everything else.

Dissent is dismissed
as attitude.
Power remains
unchallenged,

erasing emotional
tolls of discrimination,
suppressing moral outrage
with tone policing
instead of solutions.

Toxicity is normalized
to preserve
power dynamics.

Bosses silence survivors
with easy replacements.
Conformity polices
courage
out of existence.

Church

We must never
drive a wedge
between the
unchurched
and the faith.

You will be the reason
they go to hell.

Pastor has done
much good
over forty years,
and raised
a lot of money.

You will be the reason
they stop believing the Bible.

Abuse proves
we all sin,
and last week
you ate too many fries.

You will be the reason
people doubt and fall.

We are not saying
we hate you.
God wrote the message,
we just delivered it.

You will be the reason
they leave the church.

God and the church
do no harm.
Only people do.
That is why
they must be here.

You will be the reason
they question their faith.

When they lose faith,
we lose money.
Without money,
we cannot do God's work:
controlling behavior,
thoughts,
information,
and emotions,
building a world
where the powerful
always stay on top.

Bias and Privilege

Anger challenges
stereotypes
with evidence
that contradicts
beloved biases,
threatens supremacy
with neon signs
illuminating patterns
beyond doubt.

Anger disrupts
victim blaming,
makes bloody hands
boldly visible,
complicity
clear to everyone,
revealing we never
deserved our privilege.

Anger equalizes
our right
to free expression,
invites solidarity,
demands neutrality
die quickly
in the face of horrors
we recognize
in our own
reflections.

Peacekeeping

Anger threatens
group cohesion,
ripping apart peace
for the sake of truth.

Next thing you know,
everything is
out of order,
and people start to see
there's reason
to be upset.

Our culture is positive,
and anger acts
like a virus,
awakening others
to injustice
that threatens
our existence.

How immature,
how selfish
to destroy things,
humiliating us
for the sake of ethics.

It might even be
dangerous.
Violence could follow.
We might lose control
of this harmony
we've mistaken
for safety.

Fear

We might explode,
just like those people,
our greatest fears
of badness realized
for all to see.
Relationships destroyed,
maybe even our bodies,
as surely this expression
will kill us.

Plus, how do we know
how to express it?
Where it lives?
Without seeming ungrateful,
unholy, unforgiving,
irrational, dramatic,
or legitimately abandoned,
rejected and alone?

Your anger is dangerous,
violent, escalating
uncontrollably beyond
my ability to cope
with this target on my back,
this disharmony severing
connections, destroying love
and now my anger
threatens to undo me,
while I scramble desperately
for calm, privacy,
hidden places where shame
keeps us all appropriate.

Marginalization

Let confusion
fertilize self-blame
with seeds of niceness,
survival hinging
on your every kindness.

Hypervigilance
exhausts resistance
from your depleted
body, mind, and spirit,
internalizing powerlessness
at our hands,
infantilizing your instability.

Self-policing roots
in moral superiority
when those other people
get angry
while you keep your cool.
So, why unite?

Gratitude silences rage
when emotional safety
masks as physical safety,
numbing the instinct
to protect yourself.

Dominance leads you
to control your tone
until truth dissolves
under power.
Your poor little head
nestled in our wings.

Your call to be loving
plays out in personal conflict,
while systems bulldoze
your ancestors.

Your emotional vocabulary
fails you,
so you never fight back,
betraying your people,
while we whisper,
"I love you,"

until you no longer
imagine liberation
existing anywhere
outside our bars.

EXCAVATE

Finding and Excavating Anger in Our Bodies

"I have never been taught that I have a right to my anger, in the same way I have never been taught that I have a right to my body."

— LAMA ROD OWENS, *LOVE AND RAGE*

Ponderings on Excavating Anger

Anger doesn't vanish just because we were taught to hide it. It settles into the corners of our bodies and lives there, often unnoticed. Before we even realize what is happening, it becomes the tension in our shoulders, the tightness in our jaw, the ache in our gut, or the restlessness in our legs. This section is an invitation to slow down, tune in, and dig deep into the body where anger has taken root.

If the SUPPRESS section helped us recognize how and why anger has been suppressed, this one asks us to go further. It invites us to explore how anger has been buried inside us, sometimes for weeks, months, years, or decades. Anger that is not allowed to be expressed does not simply disappear. It simmers, lingers, and sometimes explodes. More often, it shows up quietly, in ways we might not immediately recognize. It can look like fatigue, headaches, digestive trouble, clenched fists, or obsessive thoughts. These are signals, and learning to recognize them is the first step in excavation.

To excavate anger, we must get curious. That might mean noticing the moment your jaw tightens and asking what story that tension holds. It might mean journaling about a knot in your stomach, listening to music that unlocks a hidden emotion, or lying on the floor and breathing into the rage that lives in your pelvis. It might mean gently asking your body where it is holding anger, and what it needs in order to release it.

Each body is different, and so is each relationship with anger. There is no one way to do this work. The practices and reflections in this section are invitations, not prescriptions. You are not broken or wrong for the ways your body holds anger. You are wise and your body is wise. This is about listening, honoring, and trusting that wisdom.

Excavation can bring surprises. You might find not only anger, but also grief, fear, shame, or memory. That is part of the process. We are not here to force anything to emerge, but to create enough safety and spaciousness for what is ready to rise. You are allowed to pause, take breaks, and reach out for support. You have choice and you get to make this process your own.

What follows are poems arising from embodied anger. They were written from the gut, jaw, tears, and fists. As you read, I invite you to let your own body speak, too. Let your sensations guide you. Let your anger show you what it has to say. Give it texture, color, sound, and breath. Let it rise to connect you with what has been hidden, as well as to make space for healing.

Body Clues

"The worst part of embodiment is being unseen."

— AKWAEKE EMEZI, *FRESHWATER*

Ponderings on Body Clues

Anger is a living, breathing force that takes shape inside our bodies through coiled jaw tension, twisted gut knots, and hidden exhaustion. For many of us, especially those of us on the margins who were taught to stay small, be quiet, or keep the peace, anger made a home in our muscle fibers, organs, and nerve endings. It learned to live in us silently, until it didn't.

This section invites you to notice, feel, and listen for the echoes of anger in the language of your body. Maybe your heart races during conflict, even when your mouth stays shut. Maybe your shoulders ache from holding everything you are not allowed to say. Maybe your belly burns when you smile through a situation that makes your whole being scream "No."

These poems and reflections are here to offer a mirror, and a way to explore how your body might be trying to get your attention. When we have been dismissed, gaslit, ignored, or punished for our anger, our bodies often carry the messages we were never allowed to speak. Tension, tightness, pain, numbness, nausea, headaches, jaw clenching, dissociation, heat, and fatigue might not *just* be physical. They might also be how your rage communicates.

We do not need to overanalyze every sensation or force stories where there are none, but it is okay to invite wonder, get curious, ask what your body might be holding, as well as what it needs to let go.

This is especially important for those of us living with intersectionality because our society does not treat all anger equally. For some of us, expressing even a fraction of our rage can lead to punishment, dismissal, or danger. So, we adapt, learn to mask it, numb it, spiritualize it, joke about it, or collapse in the face of it. Often, our bodies become the burial ground for everything we could not say out loud.

However, even when anger is buried, it does not die. It pulses, clenches, rises, and accumulates over time. It returns with headaches, stomach issues, muscle tension, fatigue, brain fog, or sudden flare-ups that seem to come out of nowhere.

In the pages that follow, you will meet the body as a storyteller of rage. You will see how anger might show up in the head and neck, shoulders and arms, gut and pelvis, hips and feet. You will see how fatigue and brain fog can be signs of long-held fire. You will feel the heat rise and maybe recognize something familiar in its burn.

What you feel is real. Your body is speaking, and it deserves to be heard with care and without judgment. May this be a space where your truth is honored and your fire is welcomed home.

Head and Neck

These throbbing temples
pound exhaustion into
tightness crossing
my forehead, burning cheeks
preceding flashing aura,
then squeezing everywhere,
thoughts halting with
eye pressure screaming
to my clenched jaw
that something is very wrong.

My ringing ears can't hear.
Tunnel vision
dizzies my overheating body,
thoughts muffled like
underwater shouting,
then racing toward puking,
mental energy threatening
to split my head open.

Eyebrows furrow and
maybe I'll finally shout,
scream, explode
everything I've ever
held back,
this tic begging me
to let shit go.

I want to yell
what no one let me say.
But my throat tightens,
air shoved out violently,
hoarseness choking coughs
where truth should live.
Neck stiffens. Muscles shake,

vibrating energy
on the edge
of coming undone.

Tears sting.
Moans knock
at the door of my mouth.
Tension blocks.
Numbness burns.
The body keeps
every word I swallowed.

Shoulders, Arms, and Hands

Shoulders hit my ears,
tightness carrying burdens
while heat meets
shoulder blades with
discontented burning,
stiffness holding captive,
as bracing keeps me still.

Sudden collapse,
anger drawing shoulders
down in suppression,
before everything clenches
to beat the living shit
out of anything nearby.

Yet, this frozen shoulder
makes me feel like
I must always hold everything,
electricity surging through
both arms, muscles flexing
when I tell them not to.
Shaking. Trembling. Vibrating.

Biceps and triceps
refuse to breathe,
tension guarding me
in both arms crossed,
stillness locking me in.

Pulling, then sudden
weakness. Heaviness.
Clenched fists follow,
fingernails mauling palms
with hot, sweaty fidgeting.
Cramping. Curling.

Then pulsing. Pounding.

Coordination slips
out through my fingertips,
numbness begging me
to grab, push, slam,
protect myself
from everything
fucktastically.

Trunk, Stomach, and Digestion

This tightening chest
shallows my breath,
everything from ribs
to sternum threatening
to burn me alive.

Lead heavy stickiness
clogs my solar plexus,
everything armored to
keep me kicking

while I yearn to
roar, scream,
exhale forcefully
from my gut into
the sealed void,
contractions pulling me
into chest vibrations,
collapsing me: a lump.

Knots churning, cramping,
punched-in-the-gut
steals my appetite as
acid gnaws with bubbling
and boiling, bloating
keeping me up at night.

Now hollowed inside,
spasms sharpen as emotions
spike into exhausted vibrations,
heartburn, then no shit,
too much shit, tightening,
and ravenous hunger
as I prepare to fight for my life.

Pelvis

Pelvis tight enough
to crush diamonds,
deep pressure
weighs in my hips.

Buzzing, pulsing,
vibrating pain,
then numbness,
as the region disappears.

Instability and tension
break through my spine,
cramps and stiffness,
trapped and silenced.

Spasms and fullness
as I bear down to
release the anger
that sears with pain
if anything dares enter.

Feeling nothing, then
everything at once,
sensitivity inflames
until I disconnect
completely.

Surges of power
tuck my pelvis under
while energy bursts
forth in rageful dancing,
reclaiming personal power
at the root.

Hips, Legs, and Feet

Unspoken anger aches
deeply in stiffened hip joints,
clicking, grinding, always
reminding, as soreness

removes flexibility,
replaced by nagging
stuckness, fatigue
taking over from
holding all of this.

Thighs vibrate
as tensions rise,
legs trembling, then
slowing with heaviness,
tightening hamstrings,
and knees screaming
from silence.

Calves cramp as news
bombards suddenly,
energy cursing for escape
before falling out,
onto the floor, into

my cold numb feet,
tingling and burning,
stomping and pounding,
destabilizing clenched toes,
ache gluing them to
unforgiving ground when
all we want to do is run.

Fatigue

Monitoring these emotions,
judging these thoughts,
suppressing these limbs
plants heavy weariness
from resisting volcanoes.

Brain shuts down,
emergency switches flip.
Sleepiness lures me
to worlds where
none of this exists.

What's the point in trying?
No amount of rest erases
sluggishness from invisibility,
drained energy from
unheard voices,
unseen days,
forgotten places.

Adrenaline crashes,
raining headaches,
body aches,
tension everywhere.
Exhaustion lets
numbness steal
the need for breath.

Sleep crashes or eludes,
trapping me in prisons
of flesh, preventing even
one cell from acting,
from doing anything at all.

Reflective Pause: Fatigue

Fatigue often emerges when anger has no outlet. When we monitor our emotions, silence our truth, or force ourselves to shrink, our bodies carry the weight of what goes unsaid. This poem reflects the bone-deep weariness that can grow from chronic suppression, especially when that suppression is both personal and systemic.

When rage is stifled and truth is swallowed in the face of injustice, burnout follows. Our bodies may shut down to protect us. Sometimes, sleep feels like the only place where we can exist without judgment, expectation, or harm.

This kind of exhaustion is a survival response, and not some indication of laziness or a poor work ethic. Fatigue often alerts us that our nervous systems are overwhelmed and pleading for a pause, release, or moment to be fully seen and heard.

Fatigue can signal the cost of not being allowed to express what needs to be said, screamed, or released with tenderness. Noticing and acknowledging this is a beautiful way to practice self-care and self-compassion.

Reflective Writing

Can you recall a time when exhaustion came out of nowhere, when your body gave out long before your to-do list did? What emotions might have been living just beneath the surface?

Write about what fatigue feels like in your body. Could anger be part of the story? What might suppressed emotions be trying to tell you now? What would it look like to listen?

Brain Fog

What am I doing here?
My pen is…
As I was saying, I
meant to fix…
What again?

All systems offline.
My truth was swallowed
by interruption
and dismissal.

Forgetfulness waves
as I struggle to find
the words. Wait…
what were we talking about?

That lightbulb over there
captured my tongue.
I feel so stupid
for that thing I said
100 times more,
after the fact.

Everything's fine. Sure.
I mean, I don't feel it at all.
When did I get here?
How?

These thoughts spew
out of order. Like you,
but I should have said…

I don't remember exactly,
over this static noise.

Just watching myself drift,
but from where, and for how long?

Heat Rising

Sudden crimson
blooms my cheeks, face,
ears, neck, scalp.
Sweat drips rage
across nearly everything.

Heat stings my eyes,
tears try to
cool the fire of my skin,

yet my chest boils
thick, hot breath,
filling my lungs,
while hives decorate
my collarbone
with exposure.

My pressure cooker
swells with the threat
of explosion, burning
everything, everywhere.

Nausea spikes
this fever with restlessness,
and restlessness dances
jitterbugs
with nowhere to go.

Thought Clues

"To pay attention, this is our endless and proper work."

— MARY OLIVER, *WHITE PINE*

Ponderings on Thought Clues

When disconnected from our bodies, we might first encounter our anger through thoughts that drift into our awareness, weaving quietly into our inner dialogue before we recognize their deeper emotional source. These thoughts can be subtle or persistent, circling our minds in quiet repetition or crashing in with urgency. They may not seem angry at first, instead seeming more like confusion, resignation, or regret. They might take the form of intrusive questions, unfinished conversations, or that nagging feeling that something is not quite right.

Our thoughts can be powerful allies in pointing us toward buried emotion, gently guiding us toward deeper self-awareness and healing. In the case of suppressed anger, our minds will sometimes try to do what our bodies are doing by holding the anger quietly, tucking it away, or wrapping it in layers of composure or justification. Even so, anger retains its own voice. It often speaks in the spaces between our thoughts, saying things like, "This isn't fair." "Why does this always happen to me?" "I should've said something." "They crossed a line." "I can't take this anymore."

Other common mental cues include ruminating or replaying events long after they happen, fantasizing about confrontation and justice, or snapping at others in ways that seem out of proportion to the moment. Sometimes these reactions feel misdirected, but they are often signals pointing toward unresolved anger. We might even find ourselves stuck in sarcasm or harsh internal monologues that mask deeper hurt.

At times, anger disguises itself as self-blame or shame. We might wonder what we did wrong, when the truth is that someone or something harmed us and we were not able to voice our hurt. We might minimize our experience by saying it was not a big deal or that we are just being sensitive. Yet, beneath that minimization lives a fire waiting to be tended. Thought clues can help us uncover that fire and begin to understand its source.

Building on the ways our minds attempt to signal unacknowledged anger, this section of the book invites you to notice and explore your thought patterns more intentionally. The poems that follow are grounded in the emotional terrain of angry thoughts and the spaces where the mind tries to alert us that something needs our attention. They serve as companions in identifying anger that is already present in the body but has not yet reached conscious awareness, even though it is very much alive in our inner world.

As you read, allow yourself to notice which lines stir something in you. What memories surface? What sensations move through your body? What thoughts do you recognize in your own internal dialogue?

The thought clues included in this book are not a comprehensive list, and your own patterns may differ depending on your life experiences. Feel free to brainstorm and write down any additional thought clues that arise as you read. Let this reflection be a doorway to deeper understanding, and a gentle entry point into the layers of your own story, where curiosity meets compassion and insight begins to unfold.

As always, move through this section at your own pace. Make space for rest and reach out for support, if needed. Excavating anger is sacred work, and you deserve care and gentleness every step of the way.

This Isn't Fair

This isn't fucking fair.
They always
get away with it,
and nobody else
deals with this.
Not like this.

I did everything
they promised
would work,
so why is
this happening?
What did I miss?

If they were
in our shoes,
it wouldn't have
gone down like this.
And if I was _____,
they would have
respected me.

Why do I always
have to be the
bigger person?
This is not what
I was promised.

They know
better, but they
still don't
do better,
and leave me
to clean up
what they

broke again.

Others wouldn't
tolerate this.
I can't accept it
as normal.
Why doesn't
it matter
when it's us?

I don't
deserve this.
They're twisting
everything to
their advantage,
yet nobody sees
or believes me.

Why Does This Always Happen to Us?

We know what this is.
Same story, different day.

We never rest,
never simply exist.
Every time hope
dares to exhale,
they pull this shit.
Nobody is coming.
Nobody hears us scream.
Our lives don't
matter to them.

How much more
can we take?

When do we get to be heard?
Instead of sacrificed for
their comfort, pleasure,
privilege, profit?

They never change,
then balk at
complaints,
roll their eyes
while we scream.

What if this were them?
They get second chances.
We get trauma, death,
imprisonment, torture,
erasure, punishment

for the audacity of
insisting on existing
with voices, souls,
and breathing hearts.

I Should've Said Something.

I can't believe I let her
treat me that way
and didn't say anything.

Why did I just take it?
She got away with it.
I froze, totally silent,
smiled and she thinks

it's okay to say that.
Probably thinks I agree.
"Why do you think it's
okay to say that?"
Perfect response,
five minutes too late.

I just couldn't get
a word in edgewise.
Talking over me.
Should've interrupted,
disrupted the peace.

I was afraid to break.
Didn't want to be difficult,
so instead I'm silenced,
truth erased, voice erased,

and thoroughly enraged
at ME. Me? Wait.
Shouldn't they be
carrying this, not me?

They Crossed a Line

I can't believe it.
That was not okay.
They went too far.
Way too far.

That felt invasive,
and they knew
exactly what
they were doing.

I did not consent.
No permission granted.
They did it anyway.
My feelings didn't matter.

They laughed. I numbed.
How much more
could I take?
They got away with it.

Disrespect made
me small.
They provoked me,
pushed harder
as I pulled away.

They calculated, coerced,
exploited and used.
My objections only
made me
easier to abuse.

Reflective Pause: They Crossed a Line

Violations often leave us stunned, our thoughts spinning as our bodies tense with anger. Whether the line crossed was physical, emotional, sexual, or spiritual, when someone crosses a boundary we didn't consent to, we experience harm. These moments can feel disorienting, especially when others ignore, minimize, or mock our pain. We might be left wondering if we imagined it, overreacted, or invited it somehow, but our bodies know and our sense of anger is often the first truth-teller.

Anger shows up to say, "That was not okay." It lets us know our dignity and humanity were not honored. Recognizing this anger is about reclaiming our voice. For many people, noticing this internal fire is the first step toward healing. When the world tries to gaslight or silence us, naming the moment for what it was becomes a revolutionary act.

Reflective Writing

Think of a time when a person or system crossed a line with you, maybe a moment you brushed off or tried to forget. What happened? How did you feel at the time? How do you feel about it now? Let your anger speak without apology or justification.

You can begin with the phrase, "That was not okay because..." and write whatever comes. Try not to edit, rationalize, or soften your words. This is your space to name the harm and reclaim your right to be outraged.

96

I Can't Take This Anymore

I am breaking.
Can't do this anymore,
carry this load alone,
holding it all together.

I am drowing.
They're piling things on,
assuming limitlessness,
but I am not okay.

I am invisible.
Inconvenient begging
for help, collapsing
but nobody cares.

I am burdened.
Dying not surviving,
running on fumes,
nearly destroyed.

I am trapped.
Everything breaking,
completely unraveling,
nobody opens the door.

Reflective Pause: I Can't Take This Anymore

Breaking points often sneak up on us quietly. We think we are doing fine until we find ourselves unable to do even one more thing. Pushing, surviving, and trying to stay strong for too long takes its toll. The load becomes too heavy, the demands too relentless, and we find ourselves overwhelmed, depleted, and fraying at the seams. Anger sometimes lives in this breaking point, masked by tears, exhaustion, and collapse. Beneath it all, there is often a righteous fury at being unseen, unsupported, and expected to carry too much for too long.

Reaching our limit does not mean we are weak. It shows that our body holds clarity and wisdom about what it can and cannot carry. It is okay to admit that we are not okay, and to acknowledge that we were never meant to carry this alone. Anger rises to defend our humanity and say, "Enough." It marks the moment when survival is no longer sustainable and signals the need for care, support, and change.

Reflective Writing

Can you remember a time when you reached a breaking point? What were the circumstances? Who or what contributed to the overwhelm? How did your body react? Give yourself space to write through the messiness of that moment.

Begin with, "I couldn't take it anymore when..." and allow your truth to spill out freely. There is no need to edit or censor what flows from the pen. Let the words come as they are. Give yourself permission to name what you carried, while honoring the voice that said it was too much.

Ruminating and Replaying

Why do I keep thinking
about this?

I should have…
Next time, I'll say…
What did they mean…
I can't believe they…

Was I overreacting?
Were they manipulative?
What if I'd said something?

The look on their faces…
I felt like a problem.
I wish I'd
stood up for myself.

Did anyone else see?
Why am I still feeling…
I can't believe I said…
What if they think…

I thought I was past this.
Every word replaying.
Why can't I sleep?
I'd do anything
to silence my brain.

Fantasies of Confrontation and Justice

I'll torch the whole damn thing—
they won't even see it coming.

I'll tell them off and watch
the motherfuckers squirm.

May the shittiest shit storm
hit their intestines with destruction.

May their snot feel like lava,
and their spit erode their teeth.

Let them beg for mercy,
bow down at our feet.

They'll be sorry when
my big-ass trans-cestors get there.

Oooohhh watch out...

They don't know who I am.
They'll regret their life choices.

I'll get them back
with the force
of a thousand biting mosquitos.

May their dicks fall off,
and their hands forget to stroke them.

No, I won't actually do it.
But goddamn, don't I want to?

After all that,
just wait until the world
sees us record them.

Irritability

Shut the fuck up!
If one more person
asks me for one more thing…

Can you just fucking
do your damn job?!?

Think it the fuck through!
Everything is too much today!

Say it one more fucking time…
I dare you!

I'm done. All of it.
No more damn explaining.

Stop chewing like that!
Pick up the damn trash!

It's not fucking funny!
Leave me alone for once.

Why are the ants, the clouds,
the wind gusts, and your eyes
all setting me the fuck off?

Self-blame

It's probably my fault
and I should have known better.

Maybe I overreacted,
and if I had just stayed quiet…

I always mess things up
and shouldn't be so sensitive.

If I hadn't been difficult,
they wouldn't have done that.

I misunderstood them
and made everything too hard.

I should have been stronger
and handled it better.

I'm the common denominator.
I always take things the wrong way.

I always ruin relationships,
and I don't blame them for hating me.

I was a bad ___,
so I deserved what they did to me.

I should be more forgiving
and fix whatever is wrong with me.

Sarcasm

Wow.
Didn't see that coming.

Of course I
have to fix it.
Nobody else would.

Sure, just
ignore me.
Nothing
fucking new.

Maybe if I
lit myself on fire
they'd finally
see me.

Fucking
fantabulous.
Just what I needed.

One more thing
to tolerate
silently.

Oh yay, another
opportunity
to pretend
everything is
fucking
unicorns and
rainbows.

Must be nice
to do whatever

the fuck
and never
have consequences.

I'm fucking
shocked.

Exhausted
and still
can't be angry.

Love that for me.

Tools for Somatic Connection

"The body, not the thinking brain, is where we experience most of our pain, pleasure, and joy, and where we process most of what has happened to us."

— RESMAA MENAKEM, *MY GRANDMOTHER'S HANDS*

Ponderings on Somatic Connection

What if your body has been speaking to you all along, through tightness in your chest, clenching in your jaw, and tension that has taken up permanent residence in your shoulders? What if those sensations are not nuisances to be ignored, but sacred signals calling you back to yourself?

Throughout the EXCAVATE section of this book, we have been exploring anger from the inside out. We began by noticing where it lives in the body and then turned our attention to the thoughts that hint at what has been buried or bypassed. Now, we arrive at a part of the journey that invites deeper somatic engagement, a space where we move into feeling anger, breathing with it, and listening to its messages through the body.

Many of us were never taught how to notice our bodily sensations, let alone trust them. We were encouraged to hide pain, suppress discomfort, and keep going no matter what. Over time, we internalized the idea that our bodies were wrong, broken, or untrustworthy. For those of us who carry trauma and live with intersectionality, coming home to the body can feel like stepping into unfamiliar territory, or even enemy territory.

That is why this work must be done gently, with tenderness, consent, and support.

In this section, you will find poems that explore practices designed to help you reconnect with your body and the anger it holds. These practices include body scans, breathwork, somatic journaling, guided meditations, mirror or video exploration, curated playlists, and somatic dialogues with questions like, "What are you holding onto?" or "Where is this anger stored?"

Turning toward the body with care, curiosity, and attention is both a healing act and a form of resistance. Oppressive systems thrive when we are disconnected, numb, and obedient. Each time you pause to feel or listen instead of override, you reclaim your worth, agency, and power.

The tools offered here are not one-size-fits-all prescriptions. They are gentle, creative invitations grounded in the truth that you are the expert on your own body. Only you can determine what feels supportive, what sparks curiosity, and what feels safe enough to explore. You are free to skip anything that feels too intense and return to it later, or not at all. There is no single right way to do this work.

As you move through the poems in this section, you might notice sensations shifting, emotions rising, or energy moving. You might feel the urge to rest, breathe, cry, write, stretch, or scream. Honor what arises, let your body lead, and let this practice become your own.

If at any point the process feels overwhelming, take a moment to pause and breathe. Remember that you are not alone on this journey. Support is available, and reaching out to a trusted therapist, healing practitioner, or friend can help you feel grounded and held as you navigate this sacred work.

May this section offer you pathways to deeper connection with your body. May it help you uncover the stories your muscles, bones, and breath have been holding. May your anger shift from something feared and suppressed to a wise and steady companion walking beside you on the path to healing and transformation.

Body Scan

Quietly,
I shut the door,
curiosity rising
tenderly,
gently.

Head:
heat,
tingling,
pressure
or tension?
A storm
behind my eyes?
Clenching
my jaw?

Neck and shoulders:
tightness,
tingling,
armored
and holding?
What didn't I
get to say
or do?

Arms and hands:
heat,
pressure,
hollow
or pounding?
Burning
to get out,
or shrinking
further in?

Belly and gut:
churning,
knots,
nausea
or weight?
What am I
swallowing,
or holding down?

Hips, legs, feet:
grounding,
tension,
urges
to flee
or stomp?
Am I trying
to run,
freeze,
please,
stand tall?

Pause.
Breathe.
Name
sensations.
No need
to fix.
Let's simply
be.

Let's wonder:
What is this
about?

Is it rage
or frustration?
What boundary
was crossed?

What truth
lies beneath
this tension
and heat?

May our hands
rest wherever
care is needed,
settle gently,
listening,
simply choosing
to be there.

Breathe again.
Be here.

Reflective Pause: Body Scan

Our bodies often carry the stories our words never had the chance to tell, and this poem gently invites us to come back home to ourselves with tender curiosity. When we slow down and scan ourselves from head to toe, we begin to uncover long-ignored sensations. For many of us, those sensations are the first hints that anger has been quietly living within us, waiting for acknowledgment. The clenched jaw, twisted belly, and aching shoulders can all indicate anger whispering for us to listen.

The act of scanning our bodies with compassion is an act of resistance in a world that often teaches us to disconnect. Many of us were conditioned to suppress or spiritually bypass our anger, to ignore what our bodies are trying to communicate. Yet, our bodies hold truth, memory, and emotion that never had the space to be processed. When we create time to notice, we offer ourselves the chance to release, understand, and reconnect.

Reflective Writing

Find a quiet space where you can sit or lie down and begin a gentle body scan. Notice what you feel in each part of your body, without trying to change it.

When you're ready, write about your findings. What sensations stood out to you? Were there areas of tension, heat, or numbness? What might your body be trying to say? Is there a boundary that was crossed or a moment of silence that deserves to be named? Let your writing flow without judgment, listening to honor what arises.

Mirror

Quiet mirror,
do you feel safe
seeing
all of me
here with you?

I ground my feet,
breathe kindly
into the space
between us.

Hold me safe
as I gaze
into my eyes,
offering tender
loving care
for whatever
I find here.

Hello, dear one.
I am here with you,
and I stay.

Is there anger?
What am I
holding in?
What words
remain unspoken?
What actions
go undone?
Where am I
disrespected,
threatened,
tired of
pretending

everything awful
is fine?

Let me gently see
all of you,
the gripping,
clenching,
expressions,
pressing,
spasms
offering clues.

You hold tension.
You deserve
so much more.

You carry pain,
buried in silence,
and fire
begging to speak.

Let truth
flow here.

I am angry they...
I am mad I have to...
I am enraged because...
I resent how much...

Let the tears,
the trembling,
the heat,
the screaming
be welcome here.
And breathe.

Look into
your eyes and say:

"I'm still here.
You are allowed
to feel this."

Let your hands
hug you gently,
arms wrapping around,

thanking yourself
for sharing,
for caring,
for being here
without hiding.

You matter always,
even when,
especially when
you are angry.

Video

Privacy please,
video just for me,
wondering
what my therapist sees.

I want to know
what I've been
holding in.

I give myself
permission today
to feel
what needs
feeling today.

Press record.
Begin to speak:

I don't even know
what I'm feeling,
but here I am...

Something
happened.

I don't feel
okay right now
because...

Let it flow.
Ramble, vent,
cry, yell,
whisper.

Tangents happen:
I'm sick of...
I wish I said...
They don't
understand...

Finally,
it surfaces.

I am angry.
That crossed a line.
This hurts.
It's fucked up.
Time to scream.

End recording.

Can I safely
play it back?

When I do,
I see tears,
clenched fists,
tension, voice,
power, fire.

It's valid.
It makes sense.
I had every right.
Feeling this way
is alright.

I'm glad I did
this tonight.
Delete. Breathe.
Knowing
I'm welcome
to repeat.

Somatic Journaling

Journal? Check.
Candle? Check.
Quiet? Check.

Heart breaths,
arms wrapped
around myself.
Begin.

What am I
feeling
in this body
right now?
Write.

Where is
tension, heat,
clenching, pulsing,
heaviness, chill,
stillness?
Note it.

Describe:
sharp, dull, prickly,
molten, frozen,
trembling, electric.
Observe.

Metaphors:
volcano,
too-tight vest,
belt squeezing skull,
sparks in fists.
List them.

What's known?

I am heaviness,
cold in the
solar plexus.
I know…

I am tension
in your toes.
Here
because…

I am the pounding
in your head,
louder each time
you stay silent.

Let words flow.

Emotion
If named,
what is it?
Anger. Rage.

Complexity
Grief, fear,
moaning
sorrow.

The pen speaks.

Story
What boundary crossed?
What was swallowed?
What feels unjust?

If this body
could move,

what would it say?

Set truth free.

Compassion
I'm listening.
You don't
carry this alone.

Thank you for
protecting,
trusting,
and sharing
your sensations
and truths today.

Breathwork

Let yourself
feel supported,
held here,
feet grounded,
body in chair.

Heart space
rises to mind
as hands
rest gently there.

Breath flows
gently, freely,
easily through
heart spaces.

Settle here awhile.

Notice
bubbling up,
suppressed concerns
rising for witness.

Irritation, tension,
frustration, rage.
What's asking,
begging to be seen?

Subtle signals:
quiet dissonance,
restlessness, images,
unspoken words.

Desire shifts,
pulling away,

tightness, heat,
lump in throat,
stinging eyes.

Acknowledge:
it's okay.

Breathe through
the heart,
inviting wisdom
to rise.

What truth
does the heart
most long
to speak?

What response
brings back
alignment,
and flame?

Welcome, anger.
You belong.

Somatic Conversation

Fatigue, tension,
silence and fear
invite me to
connect with you here.

Body, where do you feel
discomfort, pressure,
heat, tension, pain?

Maybe jaw, chest,
fists, belly, throat,
glutes, hips.

My hand rests,
listening, asking
what you are holding,
what you want
me to know,
and how long
every cell has been
carrying this.

Welcome, welcome,
surface, surface.
Words, colors,
memories, emotions.

Wonder, wonder,
what you're carefully
protecting me from,
or if you're even mine,
how I can help you
feel heard, or offer
you a lifeline.

Want to let your
story out?
No pressure either way.
I am here to
hold you,
either way today.

I never said how much
that hurt me,
and I am angry
because it was wrong,
I rage for the
injustice, and
I want it
fucking gone!

Yes, I hear you,
I'm right with you,
sharing space.

What can we do
to make this world
a kinder place?

Reflective Pause: Somatic Conversation

Sometimes the body holds what the mind is not yet ready to speak. Tension, numbness, heaviness, fatigue, or strange sensations can be messengers of unspoken or unacknowledged anger. A somatic conversation is a gentle, curious practice of checking in with the body to ask what it knows, carries, and needs.

By slowing down and tuning in to our physical sensations, we open the door to connection. Our bodies might speak in images, colors, memories, metaphors, or sudden waves of emotion. They might hold long-buried truths, protest, or grief. They might share the rage of a younger self who never got to say, "That wasn't okay." When we listen without judgment or urgency, we begin to build trust within ourselves, one moment at a time.

Reflective Writing

Find a quiet space and settle into your body. Breathe. When you feel ready, begin a somatic conversation on the page. You might write:

"Body, where are you holding tension? What do you want me to know?"

Notice any words, emotions, or sensations that arise. You might write responses from different parts of your body or focus on one area that seems to be asking for attention. Let this be a conversation grounded in compassion. If emotions arise, let them. If nothing comes up, that is information, too.

There is no need to edit or censor yourself. This is a space for honesty, however it shows up. Let your body speak, and let your anger be known.

Guided Meditation

Heavy coldness
in my core
exhausts
every part of me.

Let light flow
through the crown
of my head
to my toes,
bathing each cell
in cozy warmth.

Roots grow
to Earth's core,
where energy
lives,

recycled for good,
making it safe
for anything
to emerge.

Let healing light
perceive,
soak,
find the heaviness,

and listen,
letting it be
whatever
it needs to be.

Loud or soft.
Grief or rage.
Demanding,

fawning,
needing,
offering.

Healing light
offers loving hands,
gratefully carrying
anything heavy

to Earth's center,
where it transforms,
and words emerge.

Saying?

Thank you
for keeping
me safe.

You are allowed
to be here.

You are sacred.

I will always
listen to you
and welcome you.

Music

Power to the People,
Fight the Power,
Fuck the Police,
Get Up, Stand Up,
The Revolution
Will Not be Televised,
Say it Loud,
Say Her Name.

Where the words
meet my body,
what does
each part
say today?

Sudden tears,
move and shout.
Images each note
pulls out.

Say it. Yell it!
Fuck the…
It's all shit!

And punch out,
clench fists,
kick, shake,
stretch, ROAR!

Injustice is real,
resentment matters,
rage gets voice,
layers and layers
give choice.

Reflective Pause: Music

Music holds power. With so much injustice in the world, the right playlist has the power to speak deeply to us, move us, meet us, validate us, and prompt us to seek social change. The songs we turn to in our anger often reflect something within us that wants and needs to yell, cry, stomp, and resist. Lyrics become protest as our anger takes shape through rhythm, melody, and vibration. Through music, our fury's embodiment is made known to us. It pulls rage from our bellies, throats, and fists, channeling it outward in ways that feel grounding and liberating.

Whether we are blasting protest anthems, screaming along with punk, or swaying to soulful cries for justice, music helps us feel less alone. It reminds us that others have felt what we feel, that they are still here, and that we do not have to carry our rage in silence or isolation. Through song, anger transforms into solidarity, connection, and release. The beat helps us move anger through our bodies. The lyrics help us name it, and the shared experience helps us carry it together.

Reflective Writing

What songs express your anger? Create an anger-themed playlist or revisit one you already have. As you listen, notice what sensations arise in your body. What does your jaw do? Your fists? Your feet?

Choose one song that moves you or taps into your anger. Play it while writing, and begin with, "This song reminds me that..." Let the rhythm lead your pen. Let your words be messy, raw, and loud if they need to be. What does your body want to say through the music?

Movies

The Hate U Give,
Pussy Riot,
Stonewall,
Selma,
Hidden Figures,
Medium Cool,
The Black Panthers.

Polite family,
clenched jaw.

White fragility,
clenched fist.

Gaslit and hit,
knotted stomach.

Whose pain
is activating
mine?

I fucking hate
that character.
If I saw them
on the street,
I would....

I remember
that one time
at the park
when this
white lady...

What is
happening

inside of me?

Is there
anything
that comforts me?

How do I
feel now?

Shake,
head to toe.
Scream, yell,
jump it out!

Grab a pen,
let's talk it out.

Attention

Listen.
Pay attention.
Thoughts happen.

Sarcasm snaps
silently inside,
muttering under
my breath,
suddenly judging,
numbing, walls rising.

I should've said
something when
they crossed the line.
I feel stupid.
Fine. Whatever.
I don't care.

What do you
really want to say?

Instant no's,
gut punches,
rage, shutdowns.

I hated them
as soon as I saw them.

Forget it.
I won't answer.

Fuck the person
who drinks tea
that way.

It's fine.
I don't know
what to say.

Wait.
What lies
beneath that?

Hey self,
hey hey,
it's okay.
You are
protecting me.

That hurt.
It was tough.
You make
a good point.

I'm glad you
trusted me enough
to share today.

You matter,
and I am still
listening.

EMBRACE

Identifying and Embracing Anger in All Its Forms

"Anger is loaded with information and energy. It is a powerful tool for survival and for change."

— AUDRE LORDE, *THE USES OF ANGER*

Ponderings on Embracing Anger

What if the part of you you've been taught to silence is the very thing trying to save you?

For years, I thought I had become emotionally healthy because I no longer got visibly angry. As a child, my anger sometimes came out in loud outbursts, as children's anger often does. But somewhere along the way, I learned that growing up meant quieting down. I began to associate emotional stillness with maturity. I saw calm as strength, even when it was quietly covering grief, disappointment, and betrayal.

Then, in my thirties, I sat in a therapy session where my therapist gently said, "Hurt is a form of anger." She showed me a graphic of emotions commonly associated with anger, and I was stunned by how much of myself I saw reflected there. I suddenly saw my anger hiding in plain sight, masked as hurt, swallowed as irritation, deflected as sarcasm, or buried under resentment. I hadn't outgrown anger. I had buried it so deeply that I no longer recognized it for what it was.

Now, I notice many of my clients grappling with similar patterns. As a provider of healing services for survivors of human trafficking, I often witness people overlooking their own anger until nuance is introduced. When we begin to name specific emotions, such as feeling dismissed, irritated, or betrayed, it opens the door to deeper understanding and healing.

This section invites you to embrace the full spectrum of anger without shame. You will encounter poems that name anger in its softest whispers and its most guttural cries. My hope is that these poems offer you permission to explore the full breadth of your anger, including the quieter, more suppressed, or socially stigmatized expressions that are so often dismissed or internalized.

In this exploration, you might be surprised to discover how many of your feelings belong to the anger family. Frustration, devastation, jealousy, betrayal, bitterness, exasperation, and sarcasm are all expressions of anger. When we begin to name these nuances, we not only deepen our awareness, but we begin to see through the lies we have been told about what anger is and who is allowed to feel it.

Some of the most powerful expressions of anger are those that have been labeled too much, too dangerous, or too disruptive. Fury, in particular, deserves our attention and respect. It is a potent force that often emerges in the face of injustice, signaling where deep change is needed. Anger can also manifest as the ache of betrayal, the heat of indignation, the sting of being dismissed, the cold of disappointment, and the slow burn of injustice. These potent forms of anger often illuminate the precise places where transformation is most needed.

Some forms of anger are viewed as socially acceptable, even admirable, particularly when they align with dominant norms. However, other expressions of anger are heavily stigmatized, especially when voiced by people who live on the margins.

A white woman expressing righteous outrage may be called passionate, while a Black woman showing the same anger is often labeled aggressive, threatening, or unprofessional. A disabled person who voices frustration about inaccessible healthcare may be seen as difficult or unreasonable. A fat person naming discrimination may be told they are just making excuses or being unhealthy. A trans person expressing emotional pain may be mischaracterized as unstable or threatening.

These double standards reveal how systemic oppression shapes whose anger is allowed and whose is silenced. The systems that seek to suppress our anger do not treat all anger equally. They punish the anger that threatens power and reward the kind that upholds it.

By embracing the many faces of anger, we can begin to understand ourselves more fully and reclaim the parts we were taught to reject. Each emotion you name becomes a key to unlocking your truth. Each word becomes a step toward freedom. May this section help you recognize the anger you carry, and may it be a mirror that reflects your worth, your power, and your right to take up space.

Hurt

Tangled in pain,
wounds rise
unacknowledged,
minimized, repeated.

Dismissed, forgotten,
used, knowing
a beloved truly
did not care.

Sensitive tears,
angry in a sad,
heartbroken
kind of way.

Easily triggered,
wondering why
disappointment
burns so hot,

knowing I never
ever would have,
if the tables
were turned.

Throat tight,
words stuck,
As my chest aches,
heart hollow,
shoulders slumping
to my coiled
stomach
for all the words
I never got to say.

Annoyed

Low-level sparks
brew friction,
grating against
every need,
rhythm, respect.

Mosquito-buzzing
irritability until
finally I
SNAP,

Every little thing
too much,
eyes rolling,
sighs extolling
fantasies of escape.

No big deal,
this overstimulated
disrespect, but
I'll get them back
with chirping
fire alarms.

Jaw tight, grinding
fight, hands
restlessly wandering
to my eye twitching,
shoulders buzzing
to find space.

Impatient

Hurry the fuck up.
This unmet urgency,
trapped in slowness,
fucking inefficiency,
unwanted delay,
and pressure mounting
with no release,
and no help on the way.

Tight, restless urgency
desires an end
to this madness,
make it go away.
Internal growling
makes this line creep,
this light keep,
their mouth continue
yapping so long,
change like molasses
says, "It's not long."

Fuck compassion.
Move things along!
My hands tapping,
legs bouncing,
feet hungering to flee.

Chest compressed,
lips tight, brows
betraying my need
to urgently flee.

Agitated

Overwhelm and urgency
stir restless energy
when everything feels
so profoundly OFF.

Too much noise,
too many tasks,
all these relentless
demands
closing in on me,
trapping me in chaos.

My skin buzzes,
overstimulated,
snapping before I even
know what's wrong.

The clock ticking,
lips smacking,
his noisy-ass
chewing.

And that call,
when a text
would have sufficed.

The unsettled humming
tortures my nerves,
prickling skin,
shoulders drawn tight,
chest pounding,
stomach clenched,
my whole body
fucking keyed up.

Resentful

Anger mounts,
burning quietly
with every boundary
violated,
every need
ignored,
every moment of
exploitation.

I'm taken
advantage of.

Unseen.
Unappreciated.
Why am I
always the one?
Don't they notice
all I give?

Silently giving,
marking down
the score,
stuck and unwilling,
torn between
retreating
or violently
erupting,
dragging these
fucking chains.

Back aching,
weighed down
by this
impossible load.

Jaw clenching,
chest closing,
gut tightening
up through
my throat
with words
unsaid.

Defensive

Don't you know
who I am?

Your criticism
threatens to undo
every vulnerability.

Exposed, judged,
my armor flashes
between your
cruel words
and my dignity
and safety
today.

Argue, deny,
deflect, not knowing
what even needs
defending.
Accused, attacked,
and deeply
misunderstood.

Excuse me,
let me explain.

No, it wasn't
that way.
I'm good,
mean well,
I've got it right.

Competent innocence
lands like blows
to my gut,

face flushed,
eyes darting,
arms crossed,
shoulders lifted,
breath fast
to protect me
from you.

Angry

Felt to the core.
Forcefully,
something is
desperately wrong.

Boundary crossed.
Values violated.
Harm witnessed.
Hurt experienced.

Direct, focused,
righteous,
I am ready to
act, speak,
protect, correct.

Injustice and
disrespect has
clearly, wrongfully
been done.

Every cell awakens,
standing alert,
awake, totally
fucking done.

Speak, confront, stop!
Shaky, powerful,
expression allowed.

Hands clenched,
jaw jutting,
voice loud,
spine straight,

breath strong,
full chest
driven to catalyze
effective change.

Upset

Confusion
vulnerably swirls
with intensity,
clarity eluding
all explanations
of turbulence.

Sadness and anxiety
overwhelm what
surfaces when
something in me
knows it doesn't
quite feel right.
Something is
very, very wrong.

I'm just upset.
Words elude,
but tears flood
my frantic heart,
tenderness wondering
if overreacting is
better than
shutting down.

Throat wobbly,
stuffing down cries
to my chest
rising without release,
nausea threatening
these blurry eyes,
and then
my knees go weak.

Indignant

Moral righteousness,
dignity, and these
core values
differentiate me
from your
sorry ass.

Insult, injustice,
moral violation.
Equity on the line.
Disrespected,
treated as lesser,
burning to defend
all that is right.

Offended, appalled,
deeply wronged.
How the fuck
dare they?
Unacceptable.
I will NOT
stand for this.

Who else sees
this injustice?

Spine rigid
with every bit
of dignity,
hands square
on my hips,
lips pursed,
anchoring my
furrowed brow,

fire in my belly
saying—

Get the FUCK
OUT OF MY WAY!

Reflective Pause: Indignation

Indignation flares when a clear moral line is crossed or when human dignity is dismissed and no one speaks up. It rises in the spaces where silence enables harm, where our core values cry out to be honored and defended. Unlike silent rage or brooding frustration, indignation burns with clarity. It is a fierce moral passion that refuses to be ignored.

This feeling often comes with a deep sense of purpose, the knowing in your bones that what happened was absolutely, unequivocally wrong. Indignation might show up as heat in your chest, a surge of energy in your limbs, or a grounded, unshakable stance in your body. It can arrive as the impulse to shout, confront, or organize. Indignation does not hide. It calls us to act, speak, and align with what we know is right, especially when others will not.

In a world that rewards compliance with oppressive systems and punishes dissent, especially from those of us on the margins, indignation is a bold refusal to normalize harm. It is rooted in love and a force for justice. Honoring our indignation connects us with others who see what we see, feel what we feel, and are ready to rise, together.

Reflective Writing

Think of a time when you felt a strong sense of indignation. What was the situation? What value or principle was violated? How did your body respond?

Write freely, without censoring yourself. You might begin with, "I could not believe it when..." or "What mattered most to me was..." Let your words affirm your experience. Let them rise, just like your fire.

Hostile

Defense, dominance,
chase you away,
intimidation
threatening protection
the hard way.

Aggressive sharpness
offers meanness
as shelter
when softness
feels unsafe.

Ready to belittle,
dismiss, snap.
DON'T TRY ME.
I'll show you mean
until you wish
you never—

Untouchable,
in control,
eyes narrowed.

Mouth curled,
fist tight,
gut braced
for preemptive strike.

(I'm vulnerable inside.
Trauma set me up
to lash out in fear,
protecting unmet needs
for safety, security.)

Exasperated

Repetition, futility,
incompetence.
Tried and failed,
frustration repeated,
exhausting every ounce
of energy in me.

No more.

How many times
have I asked you
to use the right
pronouns?
Clean the fridge?
Mow the lawn?
Stop being a dick?

Nothing changes.
Circular talk
wrings the last
of my patience.

Broken systems,
emotional labor
always, always,
always unseen.

Fed up. Tired.
Can't keep going
like this. Sigh.
Throw up hands,
walk away, energy
leaking slow.

They are so fucking
absurd. Don't they see?

Sarcasm,
then flatness,
then clarity
sharp enough
to cut the whole
system away.

Tension headache
reminds me of
invisible backpacks
of bricks, carried
daily.

Groans hold back
screams.
Chest sunken
with steam.
Hands
grip my hair,
wondering if
I must surrender.

Embittered

This grief,
disillusionment,
long-brewing decay
erodes emotion
with every fence,
every wall
never repaired,
every injury
unacknowledged.

Pain calcifies
into cynicism.
Hope erodes
because
nothing changes,
they never learn,
so why should
I care?

Hardened, numb,
distrustful.
Indifferent.
Fuck your
joyful idealism.
This is my baseline.

Tongue dry,
sour taste
makes my
eyes distant,
like rot in my back,
compression
in my heart,
heaviness

offered to
every step
toward where
I've already been.

Irate

EXPLOSION.
Volcanic lava
demands action
right NOW.

I've lost
all control,
faster than
I could see.

Maximum force,
raw need,
something is
ALL WRONG.

No restraint.
Sirens blare.
Everything here
is completely
UNACCEPTABLE.

Fast.
Hot.
Boiling.
Yelling, slamming,
throwing, trembling—
UNCONTROLLABLE.

Hear and heed.
My burning face,
this pulsing vein,
my pounding heart,
this fist restrained,
threatening the world

with buzzing energy
begging to go
SOMEWHERE.

Sarcastic

Disguised vulnerability
wrapped in wit,
offering mockery.
Anger smirking.
Let me indirectly
show frustration,
contempt, powerlessness.

Exaggerated humor,
irony sharp as glass,
because I don't feel
safe enough
to be direct.

Biting comments
posed as jokes.
Watch me roll eyes.
Only kidding.

You hear me
when it stings.
Too loud,
too sharp,
too much.

If I must be nice,
I'll explode.

Jab. Relief.
You ask
if I'm serious.

Mouth twists.
Eyes dart.
Shoulders shrug.

Whatever.

Throat tight
with unsaid words,
belly fluttering
with shame.

Controlled

Restrained.
Professional.
Anger must
never leak.
Rigid lockdown
holds fury.

Calm, cool, collected.
Polite survival.
Tightly managed
simmering avoids
detection, consequence,
vulnerability.

Inside, I'm shredding
your fucking face,
but this sweet smile
won't let you see.

Clipped words
whisper logic
until fatigue.
Withdrawal.
Isolation.
Illness.

But I'm fine.

Diaphragm frozen,
shallow breaths.
Aching back,
blank face.
Sore neck,
locked in place.

Hands folded,
peacefully posed.

Jealous

Longing,
comparison,
and this aching
sense of pervasive
scarcity.

Everything
I want,
is one
centimeter
too far away.

This irritated
tension
and criticism
of your
celebration

makes me wonder.
Why you, not me?
You don't
deserve it
the way
we do.

My inadequacy.
Like, what
am I missing?
What have I
done wrong?

Maybe I'm
just wrong,
the reason
why I am

always excluded.
Internalized
oppression.

I want to smile,
but your photos
only make me
hate you more.

My heart tightens,
this stabbing
going directly
to my flushed
cheeks and
forced smile,

hunger and tension
drawing my eyes
to everything
I wish was
in my life,

fingers clenching,
hands reaching,
with every ounce
of energy restrained.

Disgusted

Angry repulsion
rises against
wrongs,
this toxic,
immoral soup of
contamination
threatens our ethics,
physicality,
and emotions.

Get that bullshit
away from me!

No!

With my full
fucking throat.
I draw the line here,
watch me go!

I am sickened,
appalled,
grossed out,
physically
recoiling,
charged with
urgency
to disconnect
from this cruelty,
abuse,
manipulation,
hypocrisy,
your ongoing
violations
of dignity.

Fuck off!

My lip curls
around my
dry tongue,
stomach ready
to hurl,
throat gagging,
skin crawling,
twitching,
as my face
recoils.

Offended

My identity
and dignity
do not stand
for disrespect.

Your insults expose
your fuckery,
and everything
you refuse see.

You've done it now,
crossed a line.
Don't you ever
speak to me
that way.

I'm stung, startled,
emotionally slapped.

Excuse me?
Completely
uncalled for.

Our values clash,
we're not the same.

Your mocking
dismissal
stops me cold,
with hot cheeks.

This anger replays
and I think
of all I could have,
should have said.

Everything is
twitching, itching,
tense and braced,
pulling in.

I'm armored,
head held high,
pushing you away,

eyes squinting
your ill intentions
real fucking
far away.

Frustrated

Stop signs.
Roadblocks.
Slowing progress.
Striving to finally
make it fucking work.

If I just try harder...
Irritation building.
Dead ends.
Miscommunications.
Delays. Obstacles. Walls.
Exploding inside.

Come on.
Why the fuck
won't this work?
No way this
should be
so hard.

Give up. Explode.

Snippy. Controlling.
But I feel helpless
to get there.
Like never.

Arms slam.
Jaw clenched.
Huffing. Puffing.
Grinding. Straining.
Stomping. Tapping.
Shaking.

Wanting momentum.
Still.
Stuck.
On.
Square.
One.

Reflective Pause: Frustrated

Frustration rises quickly when we have tried and tried again. Instead of progress, we are met with barriers, delays, or constant miscommunication. When everything feels hard and nothing seems to work, frustration can erupt in our bodies as restlessness, tension, or outbursts.

This anger signals that something is blocking your path, and that obstacle deserves to be named and addressed. It shows up in clenched jaws, stomped feet, and exasperated sighs. Frustration is not the same thing as failure. Rather, it is a signal that you care, are striving toward something meaningful, and deserve to have your effort met with support rather than resistance or silence.

It is okay to feel frustrated and to want things to be easier. When we allow our frustration to speak rather than forcing it to quiet down, we begin to recognize what lives underneath it—unmet needs, hopes, and desires that fuel our anger, a desire for progress, change, connection, fairness, or simply a break from the pressure.

Reflective Writing

Name a recent moment when you felt frustrated. What were you hoping for or working toward? What made the process feel so difficult or stuck? What did you notice in your body as frustration grew?

Let yourself write from the heat of that moment. You might begin with, "I was just trying to..." or "All I wanted was..." Do not hold back. Let your writing make room for your struggle, your needs, and what you wish had been different.

Resentful

You keep crossing
that boundary,
using me,
making me
invisible for years.

Swallowed
resentment.
Imbalance
no one sees
but me.

Emotionally
overdrawn
every time
you take
while I give.
Again. Again.

You never
thank me.

I'm cutting
you off.
Thank me.

Grudges grow.
Every fantasy
drifts to the day
you finally see
how much
I've done.
Say it.

Throat thick
with words
I'm not
brave enough
to say.

Belly, arms
holding
everything
I never got
to release.

Eyes tired
from seeing
this bullshit,
pretending
everything
is fine.

Irritated

Spiky energy
pokes holes
in patience
relentlessly.

Enough.
I need quiet.
Right now.
Away from
noises,
questions,
messes,
interruptions.

It must stop.
Fatigue
reminds me
my needs
matter, too.

Every cell
alarms with sighs,
snaps, tension,
regret
for how I
treated you
when I just
needed space.

Leave me
alone.
STFU
for two seconds.
I need
skin to settle,

jaw to release,
eyes to ease,
ears at peace,
fingers
to breathe.

Devastated

Anger, grief
collapse me
completely,
weeping for
all that matters.

Shattered
that it happened,
wondering
how it's real,
how they
could do that.

Silence, sobs
isolate pain
when words
are too small.

Who can I blame?
Where can I
point this finger
for how

my chest hollows,
core aches,
eyes swell
with tears,
breath held,
legs barely
bear weight?

Cheated

Robbed.
So much for
time, opportunity,
trust, recognition,
truth.

Duped.
Misled.
Manipulated.
They lied.
This is oceans
from what
I signed up for.

I deserved better.
Maybe if these
thoughts
keep playing,
it will finally
make sense.

Or will
humiliation,
disbelief,
and loss
keep twisting
my gut,
stabbing
my heart,
curling me
around what
should have been?

Betrayed

Trust shattered.
Thousands of pieces
of me on this cold,
slick, shiny floor.

Shock, fury
fill what's left
of my bones.

I wonder how
I ever trusted you.
How stupid.

I want to drink
your kiss,
and rip you
to shreds
with the blades
of my words.

And then I can't.
But how could you?

Obsessively replaying.
Where did
everything
veer so far
off course?

It's like I
don't even
know you.
Or anyone.
How will I ever
take someone

at their word
again?

This heartache,
this pain,
stiffens my back,
then makes
it collapse.

Stomach hollow.
Skin cold, irritated
at the words
my throat
cannot find
the keys
to fully unlock.

Reflective Pause: Betrayed

Betrayal breaks the core of our trust, fracturing our sense of safety and distorting everything we thought we knew about someone or something. This form of anger tells the truth about harm and can help us reclaim our power in the aftermath of broken trust.

Betrayal is complex, so there may be sharpness toward the betrayer, but also inward questions. How did I not see this? Was I foolish to trust? These thoughts are normal, but they do not mean the betrayal was your fault. The responsibility lies within the act of betrayal itself.

The confusion that comes with betrayal can feel overwhelming, especially when we loved or depended on the person or system that caused harm. One of the most disorienting parts of betrayal is feeling a deep ache to be held while also needing to scream and push everything away.

Letting anger rise instead of pushing it down gives us space to name what happened, affirm that it was wrong, and begin healing. It can sharpen our boundaries, remind us that we matter, and help us rebuild trust, beginning with ourselves.

Reflective Writing

Think of a time you felt betrayed. Who or what broke your trust? What did you experience in your body, mind, and spirit? Was there a moment when you realized things were not what they seemed?

Write without editing or minimizing. You might begin with, "I trusted you when..." or "It broke something in me when..." Let your anger speak freely as a witness to the harm, and let your writing hold space for the truth.

Furious

Fuck you, dipshit.
Look me in the eyes
and listen
as I tell you
every damn thing
that needs to be said.

Urgency.
Enough
is enough
is ENOUGH.
No more
walking all over me.

This changes today.
I demand better.

Now.
Or never.
Then bye.

This lava
is about to burst.
Best believe
my dignity,
boundaries,
loved ones
will be respected.

You will rue
the fucking day
you dared.

Oh yes,
you'll never forget

the way I woke you
from your bullshit.

My head
pounding
with the force
my fists wish
they could strike.
Ribs tight,
unable to contain.
Legs aching to stomp.
Voice rising, cracking,
commanding attention
with every word.

Bitter

My sarcasm
cuts with
quiet contempt
for disappointment
unacknowledged.

Anger turns
outward, barbed
with jagged edges,
refusing to move on

without closure,
some sense of safety,
a way for things
to be made right.

Hold my truth bomb,
robed in venom,
scorn, superiority
dripping from my lips.

I hope you choke on it.
I don't fucking care
if you understand.
That shit is done.

This bitter taste,
rigid jaw,
offers words
spiced in acid.
Contractions raise
shoulders against
threat from past
vulnerability.

Kindly fuck
right off.

Enraged

Intense, primal
explosions
override sense,
roaring wildfire
erupting in violence,

breaching containment.
Five-alarm overload.
Powerless. Violated.
Cornered and—
SNAP.

Hijacked
on the corner
of angry
and uncontrolled.
Every urge
to destroy,
hurt,
burn it all down.

Shaking. Sobbing.
Screaming. Striking.
Finally numb.
Fear. Shame.
Unwanted. Alone.

Everything flooded.
What did I do?
Everything throbs
in the face
of what I let loose.
This breath gasps
for survival
in the wake

of catastrophe.

Yet if honored
safely,
I find release
under this
blanket of emotion,
where power
is reclaimed.
Again.

Infuriated

I demand change.
Right now.

This minute,
an explosion
in the face
of injustice.

Protests. Marches.
Whistleblowing.
Public confrontation.

Every bullshit thing
called out
with heat
and clarity.

You've gone
too far
this time.

Hear me roar.
Watch me confront,
expose it all.

I'm in control.
Listen up.
Eyes locked.
Hands cutting air.
Legs steady,
spine straight.

For truth.
For accountability.
For justice,
for *all*.

Livid

Cold, rigid
intensity feels
volcanic, yet
strangely contained.

Boiling underneath,
terrifying and controlled.

So hot it freezes.
Rage held by will
with tight, silent,
deadly, eerie calm.

Everything severely
unacceptable has
locked me,
frozen me into
containment,
lest combustion
blow us both away.

Clipped tones.
I'm fine. Go away.
Don't talk to me.
Never forget this.

Expressionless and frozen,
tense and bracing,
danger in quiet,
so you know
not to test me.

Jaw clenched
to aching,
teeth grinding,

shoulders
back and locked,
chest like armor,
eyes,
a cold stare,
hands gripping
to keep from
losing control
completely.

Seething

Slow burning silence
simmers suppression
secretly, internally.

Explosive,
just beneath
the surface.

Privately
expressionless,
repression coils,
replays, growing hotter
with every word unsaid
as I carefully hold it together.

Permanent bracing
contains what I
really think when
I can't afford to
explode.

My calm façade
shouldn't fool you
with my heart
full of rage.

Injustice replays
stuck emotions,
boiling yet quelled.

Belly burning, roiling,
buzzing right to my
tightened throat,
my neck
pressurized,

stiffness begging

for the hot flesh
of my face, while
my buzzing
hands and feet
beg to move,
yet are jailed
by wait.

Reflective Pause: Seething

Seething is the kind of anger that simmers under the surface, quietly accumulating as we try to hold ourselves together. It is silent, controlled, and private, but far from calm. When you are seething, you might look composed on the outside, but inside your body tells a different story. Clenched jaws, tight throats, stiff necks, and burning bellies.

Seething often arises when we feel we cannot safely express what we really think. Maybe we have learned that exploding would bring consequences we cannot afford. Maybe we have been taught that staying composed is the only way to be taken seriously. So, we stay quiet, but our anger continues to build.

Seething is a form of anger that is about containment, and that containment takes a toll. Holding it in can lead to stress, sleep disturbance, chronic pain, illness, and emotional disconnection. Sometimes just noticing how seething shows up in our body can be the first step toward finding our voice again.

Reflective Writing

Think of a time when you were seething. What were you holding back? What words went unsaid? Where did you feel it in your body?

Let yourself write as though you are letting steam escape from a pressure cooker. What do you wish you had been able to say or do? What message does your body want to give you about that moment? Stay with it. Let your anger lead you to the truth.

Vengeful

Just wait.
They'll regret this
when I make them
feel what I feel.

Karmic fantasies
burn slow
while you smile
in my face.

But power
must rebalance.
You've got it coming.

This pain
returns to its source.
Your cruelty
meets my gaze.

Calculating eyes,
clenched hands,
say what my
full fucking chest
wants to scream,
standing
tall.

Wrathful

Cosmic justice,
retribution
coming for
every way
this world
is wrong.

Ordained energy
beyond me,
fury rising

rooted in
moral injury,
spiritual betrayal,
witnessed harm
so deep my soul
demands response.

Possessed
by justice's hands,
no fucks left
for what it costs.

Body shaking,
uncontained,
crying, raging, firm,
as you fear me.

Or maybe you fear
yourself,
your own
damn
consequences
arriving to bite.

You should.
Look at my
fiery center,
swirling
this body
upright,
energy beaming
from
fingers, eyes,
nose, mouth,

just in time
to save the day,
protecting us all
with disruption
of your bullshit.

Explosive

Surprise! BAM!
Reactive, impulsive,
eruptive volcano,
lava blowing
my sense away.

Breaking dams,
matches hit gasoline,
final straw sets
the whole damn fire.

Momentarily uncontrollable,
holding it together replaced
with snap, yell, slam, storm,
thunder booming through me.

I lose it, startling
all our eyes and ears
with overwhelm,
physically releasing
uncontainable explosions
blocking my breath
for far too long.

Chest pounds to bursting,
throat growls to screams,
arms flail energy away
from my roaring jaw,
trembling in overdrive
past capacity.

Outraged

Unjust, unethical
harmful, unfair,
so very wrong!

How can you
not care?!?

Morally charged,
collectively activated,
calling fucked up
as fucked up.

Unity and truth-telling.

Moral compasses
spinning wildly
when this cannot stand,
cannot be allowed.

We should all
be screaming!

Cry, yell,
post shit online,
off the cuff,
but joining
the chorus
in purpose,
body and mind.

Morals and ethics
compel words
and actions.

You say handcuffs?
Fuck it! All in.

My fiery heart
sustains courageously
wide eyes with sharp words,
conviction gesturing,
pointing, shaking,
signing, writing, resisting,
pushing my feet wildly
toward justice.

EXPRESS

Poems Expressing Anger and Ways to Release Anger

"How much anger is too much? Certainly not the anger that, for many of us, is a remembering of a self we learned to hide and quiet. It is willful and disobedient. It is survival, liberation, creativity, urgency, and vibrancy. It is a statement of need. An insistence of acknowledgment. Anger is a boundary. Anger is boundless. An opportunity for contemplation and self-awareness. It is commitment. Empathy. Self-love. Social responsibility."

— SORAYA CHEMALY, *RAGE BECOMES HER*

Ponderings on Expressing Anger

When we try to hold our anger in too long, our bodies ache with tension and our voices tremble with words unsaid. We struggle as the pressure of silence builds until it feels like we are going to snap. In those moments, intentional expression becomes a lifeline, something solid to grasp when everything feels uncertain.

Once we have recognized our anger, named it, and welcomed its many faces, the next step is learning how to express it. This section is about honoring our anger by letting it move through our bodies, voices, communities, and art, whether through words, motion, sound, action, or creative force. Here, we explore what it looks like to give anger breath, volume, and form.

We live in a world deeply invested in keeping us quiet. Systems of oppression rely on our compliance and fear what might happen if we express ourselves freely. The free, unapologetic release of anger disrupts the status quo, refuses silence, and insists on being heard. When we allow ourselves to express our rage, we also engage in powerful social resistance.

When anger is held in the body too long, it can begin to manifest as physical and emotional pain. It shows up in many ways, including chronic tension, fatigue, digestive issues, headaches, or a persistent sense of unease. The buildup can leave us feeling like pressure cookers, holding more than we were meant to, until something finally gives.

When that pressure begins to release, expression becomes essential to our well-being and sometimes to our survival. In a moment of crisis, expressive practices can offer a lifeline, helping to release over-whelming pressure and bring us back into connection with ourselves. Over time, these practices can become part of a steady rhythm of emotional care. They help us stay in touch with our anger before it builds in harmful ways. For instance, yelling, screaming, or sobbing can provide release for some people when emotions rise to the surface. Others feel a wave of release while hiking steep trails or smashing objects in a rage room. Still others find grounding in movement, paint-ing, writing, music, or satire.

The methods shared in this section are simply a sampling, not an exhaustive list. You might find that your own expressions take a different form, and that is valid and welcome. Each practice offered here is an invitation, not a prescription. Your expression is your own.

This section includes tools and reflections, as well as poems born from my own moments of fury, heartbreak, and resistance. Some were written while watching government officials strip away human rights. Others took shape in the aftermath of personal betrayals or collective grief. These poems rage against injustice, including transphobia, racism, white Christian nationalism, and systems of control that criminalize poverty, deny healthcare, erase identity, and fund war instead of collective care.

To express anger is to reclaim the breath we were taught to hold. It is to give voice to truths we were told to suppress. It is to insist that our lives, our needs, and our humanity matter. Let this section be a reminder that your anger is not a flaw or failure. It is part of your truth and deserves to be heard. It is a fire to be tended, and each time you express it with intention, you become part of a larger movement that seeks liberation, healing, and justice for us all.

Ways to Release Anger

"In truth, we have to integrate our wounds into our understanding of who we are and what we are really capable of so that we can be whole human beings. Only from there can we begin the process of healing the brokenness, the brokenheartedness within ourselves that is then the foundation for beginning to heal that in our larger society."

— REV. ANGEL KYODO WILLIAMS, *RADICAL DHARMA*

Ponderings on Releasing Anger

Anger, like grief or love, can take many forms, and each person's path to expression is deeply personal. The practices shared here focus specifically on how to give anger a path out of the body through grounded, physical, and creative releases. Whether the expression comes in a fiery surge or a slow simmer, each release is valid. What matters most is that anger is allowed to move.

Physical movement can be a powerful ally, when it is accessible. Activities like hiking, dancing, climbing, jumping, stimming, or pacing may help shake loose the tension that anger creates in the body. Some people find clarity and release through vocal expressions like yelling, screaming, groaning, or singing, which can restore a sense of agency and reconnect them with their voices. Others find release through art and creativity. Writing, painting, playing music, or using humor and satire to express anger can channel pain into something transformative.

These tools are meant for use beyond moments of crisis when release feels urgent. They can also support a consistent daily practice of honoring anger. There is no need to wait for pressure to build before responding. Instead, anger can be tended to regularly in ways that feel affirming and accessible. This intentional tending interrupts internalized cycles of anger suppression and affirms our right to be heard, acknowledged, and supported in our full emotional lives.

You might already have ways of tending to your anger that work for you, or perhaps you will discover new ones along the way. Use this section as an invitation to experiment and listen to your body. Let your expression be authentic and adaptive.

Your anger deserves space whenever it arises, not only when it threatens to overflow. As you explore what helps you release it, remember that expression is resistance, strength, and truth-telling. It is a powerful way to reclaim your voice, breath, and humanity.

Therapy

Attuned, I am safe here.
Named without minimizing.
Spoken without apology.
Resisting shifting to gratitude
or pushing away,
diverting, running, stuffing.

Sit with it. It's okay.
I am not alone,
and this caring other
has felt it, too.

Notice where it lives.
Let your tone shift
louder, sharper, trembling,
even mean. Honest.

Clench your fists.
Exhale hard.
Pause.

Feel energy rising,
therapist witnessing,
validating, not fixing.

Boundaries crossed.
Power denied.
That's right. Real.
It happened.

You are allowed to feel it.
Release it.
Punch this pillow.
Scream it
over and over and over.

Until stillness or action,
purpose and release,
validation and tears visit
without needing closure.

Massage and Energy Work

Set intentions to release.

Breathe slowly, deeply,
hidden emotions
rising in their own time.

(If they don't,
that's okay too.)

Hands placed
where emotion stirs.
Gentle touch
and no pressure.

You are safe
to cry, shake,
sigh, speak.

You are welcome
and seen here.

Anger is invited,
so let it flicker,
simmer, spark,
or simply
blink awake.

No need
to justify.
No need
to hold it back.

Breathe again,
my friend.
Let go.

The singing bowl hums.
Tones find stuck places,
nudging them loose.
Bellybutton, lips,
eyes, nostrils,
fingertips, toes.

Energy shifts
with every
breath out,
every ripple
of sound,
every quiet
second passing.

Let it move as it will,
softness embracing
every blessed release.

Rage Rooms

Smashing shit.
Yes—fucking it up!

Tape that shit
to the car.

Get pissed.
You know you are!

Suit up. Protect.
Look that motherfucker
in the face.

Rage grows louder,
breaths heavier.

Grab the damn bat—
FUCK THAT SHIT UP!

Smack the motherfucking
windows to smithereens.
Dent the bumper as you

Shout! Fucking CURSE!
Swing, throw, crack, break!

Roar. Growl.
Hit and hit, repeat, CUSS!

Smash the motherfucker
in the face until it's gone.

Move raging energy out
to give them
what they fucking deserve

until you feel a cool
vibration wave through
muscles, bones,
feet, chest, arms, mouth.

Standing in wreckage,
shaking it out,
sipping water,
exhaling everything out.

Vocalizing

Somewhere private,
standing firm, feet wide,
knees soft, jaw loose.

Breathe through your nose,
belly expanding
easy, natural.

Let energy rise,
sound moving
from gut to throat.

Growl. Howl. Roar.
Louder. Sharper.
So much messier.

Scream, sob, wail.
Sigh into the wave,
then point.
Punch. Shake.

Rinse. Repeat. Burst.
Pause. Burst. Pause.
Burst. Pause.
Pause.
Burst.

Then silence.
Breath heavy.
Spine tall.
Heart pounding,
until you
release
it all.

Reflective Pause: Vocalizing

Vocalizing is one of the most ancient and instinctive ways we release emotion. Our bodies often know before our minds do that something needs to come out. When animals are threatened, they growl or roar. When babies are distressed, they scream. Yet somewhere along the way, many of us are taught to stay quiet. We are told to be nice, to keep our voices down, to not make a scene.

Our anger deserves sound. Letting it rise from the belly through the throat and out into the open air can be one of the most powerful ways to move that energy through us. Screaming into a pillow, yelling in the car, roaring in the woods, even sighing or groaning deeply can help us reconnect with ourselves. When we do this with intention, we give our nervous systems a way to release built-up pressure and tension.

This kind of release can be messy, loud, and imperfect. That is part of what makes it beautiful. It is a full-bodied reminder that we are alive, that we have a right to take up space, and that our anger matters. When we vocalize our rage, we interrupt the silence that keeps us small and invite in a sense of freedom.

Reflective Writing

Have you ever wanted to scream but stopped yourself? What would it take to give yourself that permission?

Write about a moment when you felt like yelling but swallowed it instead. What did your body want to do? What would it sound like if you let it all out? Try putting that sound on the page. Let your words growl and roar. Let them sob and wail. Let your writing echo the power of your voice, uncensored and alive.

Shake

Shake it off,
standing tall,
feet firm,
knees bent,
shoulders dropped,
jaw loose,
joints unlocked.

Start small.
Bouncy, bouncy,
BOUNCE, bouncy,
BOUNCE, BOUNCE!

Knees and arms,
trunk and legs,
neck and head.

Bigger.
Faster.
MESSIER.

Shake it off
your hands,
your head, jaw,
shoulders
uncomposed.

Breathing rhythm,
exhaling sound
violently, anger
leaving each pore
in your skin.

Shake, shake,
Shake, SHAKE,

heaviness slowing
you gently
into stillness.

Hands on
your heart,
solar plexus,
arms, gut,
feeling
something
has shifted.

Punch

Punching bag.
Gloves on.
Strong stance.
Feet grounded.
Knees bent.
Core engaged.
Eyes locked.
Fists clenched.
Arms ready.

Inhale deep.
Charge up.
Again. Again.

Wham! Punch,
exhale sharp
with every strike.

Furrowed brow.
Tightened jaw.
Go in bursts.
Let fists flurry.

Pause. Reset.

Shout. Growl. Grunt.
Punch. PUNCH.
Drive your rage
into the bag.
Again. More.
Harder. Stronger.

Keep going! Come on!
Show the motherfucker.
Go! Go! GO!

Until,
movement stills.
Hands loosen.
Open.
Breath slows.

And you
let go.

Ripping Paper

Fuck your words.
Fuck your name.
The lies.
Those events.
Every bit
written here.

This paper
burns my hands,
filthy with grime
and your lies,
building bricks
in my hands, chest,
arms, jaw.

This one little tear
slowly destroys
every last word.

Pieces getting
smaller, ripping
loudly, violently,
deliberately destroying
every cruel word I

can't fucking stand,
the names you called,
the rights erased,
the harm done
with your full chest.

Fuck all of it.
Then flush all of it,
every last piece

so small I can't tear,
until I catch
my breath again.

Drumming

Drum, table,
floor, wall,
thighs, chest,
fingers, body.
Sit, stand,
arms loose.

Rhythm slow,
mounting, fast,
loud, wild,

heavy beats
calling anger's
rise, breathing
rhythms of fire.

Vibrations rise
loud and proud,
and I'm done!

This matters!
Fuck off!
Dipshit!

Whole body
pulses it,
sweat chasing
tears clearly

into the stillness
with one final hit.

Uncensored Writing

The first words
on my mind
are fuck you!

This paper
will not argue
like you,
will actually
listen,
let me vent
all of it out.

So here goes:

Fuck this fucking
dipshit and his
mean, nasty,
manipulative,
underhanded
"forgiveness"
and insults veiled
as repair, as words
stab my heart
beyond repair!

Fuck everything,
the white women,
the power they wield,
white supremacy,
and the fucking church
meeting on the corner!

Let it all out!
Let tie pos exist,
spelling be wrong,

grammar ain't shit.

Just go! Repeat
yourself. Fuck
him. Fuck him.
FUCK HIM!!
FUCKING FUCK HIM!

Fngers moving,
messy, loud enough
for every word
you never said,

especially the ones
unacceptable, barred,
unallowed, shameful.

I'm so fucking
angry because....

....
....

Cry, scream,
underline
energy shifts,
then burn that shit
and release it!

Scribble

Beyond words,
this aggression begs
for pens like weapons,

dragged across pages
until every surface
RIPS. Scribble

fast, tight, motion,
strokes with enraged,
furious intensity.

Fill pages upon pages,
the next, the other one,
the notebook,
the whole damn universe,

shapes emerging,
jagged lines,
spirals, slashes,
pure chaos!

Go, and go.
Do some more!!
More and more
until the hand
says stop

and the page shows
all that no longer
exists inside you.

Throw Ice

Bagged ice
numbs my hand
then shatters.

S
  H
    A
      T
       T
         E
           R
             S

All over the

T
  U
    B

In millions
of tiny pieces.
Every damn thing
I hate crashing
as I yell:

          NO!!!!
              ENOUGH!!!!
                  YOU DON'T GET TO DO THIS!!!

Faster, harder, louder,
breathing ragged,
body loose,
arms strong,
stronger, strongest,
until something

breaks open inside
and I finally release
in quiet breaths,
rest and the silence
that follows.

Unsent Angry Letters

Your name returns.
A curse
I can't spit out.

Your face flashes,
memory haunts me,
over and over,
and every time,
I wish I'd said:

Dear ass wipe,
Guilt, shame,
and public humiliation
are not the way to
capture my heart,
my friendship,
my presence in
your life.

Fuck your
manipulation,
your soaring high
joy in bringing others
down a notch.

Fuck your spoiling
the joy, your fucking
feigned innocence
and ignorance
when you have no idea
why things happened
the way they did.

You're such a victim.
Boo hoo, cry me

a fucking river.

Actually don't,
because I am
out of here and
you can fuck off
forever and to eternity.
Goodbye.

Love, No Regards,
Me.

(Every word of
that tirade loosened
the cramped muscles
between my shoulders
so now I can
BREATHE.)

Dig Dirt

Shovel, trowel,
bare hands.

Garden bed,
forest edge,
backyard zen.

Set jaw,
planted feet,
digging deep.

Rough, fast,
hard, panting,
sighing, yelling.

No more!
You do not
own me,
let alone
my peace!

Sweat, heat,
emotions rise.
Grunting, tossing,

leaves, rocks,
words to bury
under smoothed
soil, inhaling
deeply into knowing
everything's shifted.

Chop Wood

Feet wide,
knees soft,
spine strong.

Gripped firmly,
intention strikes
this one damn log

that almost looks
exactly like your face.

Rhythm and chaos
mess that shit up
with every curse
and cry

reverberating across
every joint,
breaking rage apart
piece by blessed
fucking piece

until finally,
all that's left
are smithereens
and this softened

breath releasing
what no longer lives
inside me.

Clench and Unclench

Grab that rage
and squeeze!
Then release
All.
Of.
It.

Feet, spine,
fists, jaw,
nose, ribs,
arms, legs
pelvis, the
whole damn
body. Go!

Tense, release,
build, hold,
drop and breathe.

Clench and sigh,
grunt and growl,
shake it off,
head to toe.

Roar into the Void

Roots grow deep
from my feet
to the center
of the earth,

anger gathering
weight in my belly,
breath filling every
cell with heat.

Exhaling guttural
roars into Earth's
molten core

where it is received
with fire intended
to recycle it.

Over and over,
until no rage
remains, let
it roar and roar

my chest into softness,
lungs into coolness,
jaw into ease,
shoulders into rest,

hands on my heart,
then on my belly,
feet drawing
strength and goodness
from the Earth
into every space

in need of
feeling remade.

Guttural Tones

Hold back
the path toward
epic explosions.

Find private spaces
inviting presence,
loud and free.

Let loose
and see
the way
past it
is through.

Breathe into every
nook and cranny,
filling your body
until it feels like
you might just *pop*.

Then *roar,*
grunt,
growl,
moan,
YELL!

All of it out.
Low rumbles,
shaky screams,
sharp bursts
building rhythm,
volume intensifying
with recklessness

into letting go.

Strong Exhales

Rhythmic exhales
massage anger
from every crevice
hiding energy
secretly.

Find your beat.
In through the nose.
D...E...E...P...

Exhale through the mouth.
SHARP!

HAAAAAA!!!
SHHHHHH!!!

In. OUT
In. OUT! In. OUT!

Sharper, faster,
louder, stronger,
sigh and huff.

Shoulders up,
then DOWN.
Fists clench,
then RELEASE.

One last long
e...x...h...a...l...e...

and simply be.

Paint Cuss Words

Start with a surface.
Canvas, wall, brick.
Anything that can take it.

Choose your weapons:
reds, blacks, neons,
contrasts that clash,
burn, scream.

Brushes, sponges,
your fingers,
or that loud,
satisfying palette knife.

Let it be messy.
Let it drip.
Let it almost feel
violent.

FUCK YOU,
FUCK white supremacy,
FUCK the patriarchy,
FUCK this
FUCKING shit.

Layer words.
Drip them.
Slash them.
Splatter. Smear.
Make them
mean something.

Cover lies
with moments
of unfiltered truth.

Stand in it.
Stomp. Shout.
Move with the beat
of your breath
and the brush.

Let your rage
become form.
Let the pain speak,
brushing beauty ugly.

Hang it.
Burn it.
Bury it.
Or paint over it
tomorrow.

Voice Memo Rant

This voice recorder
invites uninterrupted,
judgement free,
censorship void
release.

This first angry thought:
Why the fuck did he do that?

Leads to a cascade
spiraling into whispers,
shouts, curses, refrains
as I repeat myself. Stop.
Interrupt myself.

Change course,
pace the room, stomp,
pound, call out your name,
that other thing, and
everything I wish I'd said.

My voice breaks, shakes,
gets fierce and hoarse,
coherence going
out the window.

When my breath slows,
the rant runs dry,
calmness replaying it,
witnessing it,
deleting and releasing it.

Hiking and Climbing

This hill whispers,
calling me with fingers
to the winding trail
where the steep
rock face awaits.

Each step, intentional,
pounds anger
into the ground,
and sometimes
your face.

Every heavy exhale
releases disgust
into the soil,
where it composts
something new.

I'm done. Fuck you.
Fuck this. Fuck it.
Never fucking again!

Stop, scramble, push,
one leg and foot,
then the other,
tension pushing up

with each rock
my hands grasp,
pulling my pounding
heart up farther
than my anger
falls down.

The peak summons

my inner beast,
roaring, sighing,
crying, whispering,

as I dig the hole
where the ashes
of this fiery anger
now live, nourishing
the tall birch tree
with love.

Trampoline

Small bounces
sync body and breath,
each one higher,
harder, more fiercely
alive with rage.

Each jump exhales:
HAH! UGH! BAH!
Yells hurling out
what is no longer mine.

Arms flail, fists clenched,
hair flying wild
with every rising breath.

Up, sideways,
twisting, flipping,
cussing, dancing,
moaning, bemoaning.

Tears rising
as anger drains
in rhythm,
breath softens.

Silence lands,
embracing this
healing heart
as I lie back,
watching clouds drift by.

Creativity

Words, paint, sound,
movement, clay,
fabric, fire.

Everything now
is meant to be real.
Not so much pretty.

Frantic brushstrokes,
cruel lyrics, dissonant
chords and colors,
broken sentences.

Create chaos,
fragments, heat
rising in color,
volume, body,
voice.

Outside the lines,
screaming onstage,
overreacting, clashing
every fucking note.

Everything shifts.
Fluid.
Anger releases
through my senses
as I step back
and witness
all I have made.

Share it, burn it,
build on it, hide it,
release it.

Rage Circles

First things first:
No fixing.
No debating.
No dismissing.
No bypassing.

100% feeling.

Boundaries contain
burning herbs,
a cast circle
declaring sacred space.

All emotions welcome
without censorship,
and everything stays
here safely.

Breathe into
every twisting
buried deep within.
Let it stir.

Hold space.

Scream, shake, stomp,
weep, roar, drum,
hit, rip, tear.

Everything is welcome here.

Eyes open, hearts present,
bearing witness
as we growl,
releasing collective

primal moans,
chants rising naturally

as breath brings us home,
stillness offering bodies
space to exhale
and release.

Community

Rage needs
community,
places to break free,
speak truth,
and rise together.

This is not okay.
We all see it.
We all feel it.

Stories rise
like the sun
after storm-soaked nights.

Minimizing fades,
bypassing dissolves,
gaslighting crumbles,
shame retreats.

Together we see
we are not alone.

Validation cools
fires with tears,
laughter, silence,
mutuality,
and shared balm.

Art, spells, protest,
feet in the street, ritual.

Anger becomes fuel
for organizing,
movement,
and healing.

Nervous systems
co-regulate
to the pulse of
shared purpose,
showing up
with tenderness.

Activism

After lifetimes of silence,
activism grabs your hand
and shouts:

Your anger matters.
Your voice is needed.
Hope exists.

Naming what hurts
connects us in
shared fury
toward what matters.

Impact amplifies
in protest, petition,
art, organizing,
disruption, education.

Details clarify
what must change,
what must burn,
what must be rebuilt.

March, write, speak.
Donate, build, burn.
Shout, chant, post.

Scream into the mic.

Collective care
and justice movements
make space for your
grief, fury, exhaustion,
and voice.

Respectability dies
in favor of human rights.

Resistance becomes sacred.
Rest becomes celebration.
Healing becomes welcome.
Rhythm replaces burnout.

Reflective Pause: Activism

Activism is often a lifeline for people who have been told their voices don't matter or that their anger makes them unlovable. Stepping into activism can feel like someone finally saying, "You belong here and you are not alone."

At its best, activism channels rage into momentum, grief into solidarity, and exhaustion into shared purpose. It gives anger a voice, direction, and sense of community. From petitions to protests, organizing to art, activism helps us name injustice, demand better, and create something new. It reminds us that anger is not the opposite of love. Rather, it is frequently what protects love, fights for it, and refuses to let it be destroyed.

In a world that often rewards silence, activism is the noise of resistance. Whether you're marching in the streets, donating time or money, creating disruptive art, or teaching others, your participation matters. There is no one right way to show up. Even resting with intention can be activism when it breaks the cycle of burnout and extraction.

Reflective Writing

Start with this: What causes make you feel most alive, angry, or passionate? Then ask yourself: Have you ever used your voice in ways that felt risky but right? What happened?

If it feels supportive, reflect on a time when collective action made you feel seen, supported, or powerful. What did that stir in you?

Finally, consider: How can your anger fuel change without consuming you? What kinds of rest or care help sustain your commitment to justice?

Magic Ritual

Smoke clears the air
in spaces protected
by salt and chiming bells,
opening room
for silence.

Candles, herbs,
paper, dirt, water,
and one cauldron,
navy blue with moons,

welcome the full truth.
Curse words welcome,
tears too.

Oil and ash anoint
hands, feet, chest
as we tear, burn, bury,
returning anger's cry
to the center of the earth.

Chants, songs, spells
move energy through
and out, untangling
every tightened muscle.

Ancestors guide,
hold, and transmute rage.
It is done. I am free.
Thanks be.

Burning Shit (Safely)

Ceremonial cauldrons
welcome letters,
names, memories,
lies, labels,
injustices, systems
that must be
burnt down
before the
healing comes.

Breaths deepen
as the match ignites
every metaphorical
thorn holding me
captive.

You don't own me.
I am my own.

You don't own me.
I release you.

(Fuck off.)

Heat rises to meet
the fire in my chest,
flames consuming
every fury with
ashes, smoke,
and silence,

scattered in streams
to release them
into something
deeply good.

Sitting

Eyes close softly,
body finding stillness
in simply being alive,
spine lengthening,
shoulders melting,
as the ground below
cradles trust completely.

In through the nose,
two, three, four.

Pause,
two, three, four.

Out through the mouth,
two, three, four.

Pause,
two, three, four.

Repeat.
Inhale, pause,
exhale, pause,
knowing I am here,
breathing

into my anger,
hiding behind teeth,
curling in my gut,
clenching my fists
as they rest in my lap.

Rising, the anger
is my friend.
Rising, there is nothing

wrong with me.
Rising, it is holy
and I am holy, too.

Every exhale fans flames,
offering oxygen to dance,
presence without judgment
in simply breathing

as it grows, shifts,
weeps, trembles,
screams, grieves,
and I witness it,
befriend it.

I see you, anger.
I hear you, anger.
You are allowed, anger.
You are not too much, anger.

As my breathing slows,
my jaw unclenches,
fire softens to warmth,
anger reminding me
I am here, whole,
loved, and sacred.

Sitting, I breathe
and simply be.

Humor and Satire

Fucking furious
and absolutely absurd.

Fuck yeah, I've always
wanted to smile more
while being actively
oppressed.

Anything else I can do
to help your fucked up,
fragile ego feel safe?

Sure, take your fucking time
replying to that email
about my late payment.

Only my survival
hangs in the balance.

Nothing says ally
like a friends list of
liberal, moneyed, cishet
white women named Susan
who read *White Fragility*
once and get it now.

Yeah, all lives matter
until you deny
my existence,
flush my kid's
pronouns
down the toilet,
and defund our humanity.

Ironic, dontcha think?

Corporate Ally Barbie
finds a fucking microphone:
I love all people, especially
when they boost the quarterly
DEI report.

Meet President Dump,
who thinks gender-affirming care
is a waste of money,
while wearing orange makeup,
a toupee, and shoe lifts.

If I didn't laugh at
all the damn gaslighting,
I'd have to burn the building down.

Introducing rage meditation,
for when you need zen
but also need to scream
FUCK IT—and you too.

Fucking hell.
Things don't happen
for a reason.
WTF is the reason, Brenda?

Raise your hand
if you've ever been called
aggressive or mean
simply for existing
without apologizing for it.

Cool, cool, cool.
Everything is fine.
Let's plan the revolution
from it.

Poems Expressing Anger

"It is easy for a spiritual teacher to say, 'Give up anger.' There is reason for anger if we look at the plight of the world's children— and I don't just mean the babies, I mean all of Earth's children who are caught in war, hunger, disease, injustice. Sometimes it looks as if there's no justice anywhere in the world."

— MA JAYA SATI BHAGAVATI

Thoughts on My Angry Poems

After the first six months of Trump's second term, with the support of my therapist and massage therapist, the anger I had been stuffing down finally rose to the surface and poured through my fingertips onto the page. These poems came as a blazing fire of grief and truth. Many came to life as unfiltered lists of everything I was furious about in that moment, from systemic injustice and political cruelty to personal pain and long-held rage. With each line, I felt a little more alive. The energy of my anger processed itself in ways that were cathartic, clarifying, and freeing.

Writing these poems reminded me that anger is not the enemy. It is an energy that wants motion, purpose, and to clarify or create boundaries. It wants to be heard, expressed, and allowed to shift. Putting words to my anger gave me a sense of power and helped me move through emotions that had felt too overwhelming or frozen to touch. It did not fix everything, but it did give my emotions somewhere to go, offering a pathway for release that felt honest and healing.

As you read and reflect, I invite you to write your own angry poems. Let them be messy, loud, raw, sarcastic, bitter, or devastated. Do not worry about form, grammar, or tone. Just let the words fly however they come.

Unfiltered expressions like this can be both deeply healing and a powerful act of resistance. In a world that insists we sit quietly and behave, choosing to give voice to your rage becomes a bold declaration that your truth matters and will not be silenced. It is a refusal to comply with systems that rely on your silence to maintain control and cause harm. Through this kind of expression, we survive, heal, and begin to shape something new.

Fuck Trump

Fuck you
and your Vance,
and your Musk,
and your job,
and your broke-ass
oath you never
truly took.

Fuck you
and your stupid
fucking pen,
your passport-taking plans,
trans-hating orders,
disassembling
all that matters.

Fuck you
and your chaos,
shock and awe,
hatred, fascist
fucked up shit.

Who wants to deal with it?

Fuck you
and your xenophobic,
racist, icy orders,
money,
gestapo ways,
even in L.A.

Fuck you
and the concentration
camps where you
torture, kill, and maim,

murder dreams
and fake disdain.

Fuck you
and your perpetrating
ass, hiding Epstein
up your ass,
where your guilt
is in the past.

Fuck you
and your
witch hunts
into teachers,
banning books
and never bigots.

Fuck you
and your anti-climate-science,
white supremacist loving,
Christian nationalist adoring,
god-complex-holding ass.

Fuck you
and your border checkpoints,
pressroom purges,
loyalty lists,
health care and food erasing,
war machine building.

Fuck you
and your hunger
for power and bombs,
libraries almost gone,
and the way you always
stab the best neighbors
in the back.

Fuck you
for hating everyone
and everything that dares
question you, challenge you,
dislike you, protest you.

Fuck you
for the ways you make
hope feel naïve,
safety like a pipe dream,
and truth like a crime.

Fuck you!
But still we remember
how to burn,
how to build,
how to rise,
how to love.

Fuck you!
Now we stomp,
and we chant,
and we scream,
and we refuse to stop
or be driven by
your fear.

Fuck you!
We are bigger
than your hate
and your plans
to decimate
everything dear.

So let me be clear:
FUCK YOU!

Transphobia

Fuck your bans
on our care,
bathroom bills,
deadnaming.

Fuck you when
you say we'll always
be [insert sex] to you.

Fuck your denied
gender markers,
your proof required
for dysphoria.

Fuck the TERFs
"protecting women,"
and those missing
"the old you."

Fuck employers
who declare you're
"just not the right fit."

The misgendering,
the endless apologizing.

Fuck your assumptions
and your hate,
your intensity of debate.

Fuck transition policing,
intrusive questions,
and "biological sex,"
whatever the fuck that is.

Fuck your religion
that you weaponize
to legitimize every
ounce of hate
used to discriminate.

Fuck age restrictions
on life-saving care,
purity tests
when you pull down
underwear.

Fuck your tropes,
fuck your punchlines,
your invasive questions,
and willful ignorance.

Fuck nonbinary erasure,
calling trans folx threats
to children, demanding
investigations, justifications.

And fuck your murder
every time we see the news
and see another name like ours,
never knowing
when it will be our time.

Queerphobia

Fucking burn it down!

Queerphobic bullshit
killing lives, stealing hope,
offering endings,
but never beginnings.

Fuck love the sinner
hate the sin.

Fuck being called out
for confusing children.

Fuck bans on queer
books in schools or libraries.

Fuck conversion therapy
killing our youth.

Fuck half naked heteros
telling queers not to flaunt it.

Fuck cruel silence and stares
toward our partners and kids.

Fuck shelters and housing
kicking us on the streets.

Fuck using "That's so gay"
as an insult.

Fuck religious leaders
preaching damnation.

Fuck tokenization at Pride,
invisibility the rest of the year.

Fuck being fired, or never hired,
for not fitting the culture.

Fuck straight people
demanding our respect.

Fuck hate crimes
and silence on the news.

Fuck politicians making
our existence an issue.

Fuck friends abandoning
friends for coming out.

Fuck being called divisive
for demanding visibility.

Fuck assumptions about
queerness and trauma responses.

Fuck proving humanity to jackasses
intent on never listening.

Fuck queerphobia.
Fuck you.

Racism

Fuck the cops
murdering Black
lives with impunity.

Fuck your
"I don't see color"
when you know your
shirt is red.

Fuck tokenizing
our children to say
you're so inclusive.

Fuck schools named
after slaveholders
and confederate generals.

Fuck whitewashed
history books that make
colonizers seem kind.

Fuck calling my family
angry, aggressive or
intimidating.

Fuck voter suppression
of Black and Brown voters.

Fuck refusing to pronounce
someone's name correctly.

Fuck calling
racialized communities
bad neighborhoods.

Fuck medical racism,
unequal access to care,
and being dismissed in pain.

Fuck cultural appropriation
and cultural disrespect.

Fuck weaponizing the law
against the global majority.

Fuck generational wealth built
on stolen land,
with stolen labor.

Fuck racist mascots
defended in 2025.

Fuck assuming "diversity hire"
for your racialized boss.

Fuck the prison industrial complex
targeting Black and Brown bodies.

Fuck overpolicing and underfunding
Black, Brown, Immigrant communities.

Fuck expecting racialized people
to educate white people
at the expense of their own peace.

Xenophobia

Fuck demands for English.
Fuck mocking accents,
and asking if someone is illegal.

Fuck racial profiling,
blaming immigrants
for stealing jobs,
then exploiting their labor.

Fuck border walls,
making fun of foods, then
stealing all their recipes.

Fuck banning refugees
fleeing actual fucking wars,
then banning Black and Brown
people from entry.

Fuck demanding assimilation
and fuck denying basic belonging.

Fuck equating patriotism
with whiteness,
calling countries
"shitholes."

Fuck assuming someone
doesn't belong
because their name
doesn't sound like it
to you,
then portraying them
as threats in political ads.

Fuck ignoring trauma
from displacement,
migration, and survival.

Fuck detaining asylum seekers
and treating them like criminals.

Fuck making jokes about
"anchor babies" and "chain migration."

Fuck seeing diversity as a danger
instead of a gift,
and FUCK valuing borders
but not the lives within them.

ICE

Fuck ripping children
from parents at borders.
Fuck separating families.

Fuck putting children
in handcuffs,
toddlers in cages.

Fuck aluminum blankets and
lies about detention centers.

Fuck denying medical care,
and nonconsensual
hysterectomies.

Fuck solitary confinement
for people seeking asylum.

Fuck targeting
school drop-offs
and church services.

Fuck destroying documents
and denying abuse.

Fuck raiding homes
without warrants
in the middle of the night.

Fuck separating nursing babies
from breastfeeding parents.

Fuck ignoring asylum pleas,
deporting people to die.

Fuck mocking detainees
relentlessly behind closed doors.

Fuck placing queer and trans
immigrants in
dangerous facilities.

Fuck ankle monitors
like shackles
and treating humans
like contraband.

Fuck profiting off
private beds
and doing it
in the name of security.

Fuck ICE!

Fuck Vance

Fuck Vance!

Fuck allegiance with hate.
Fuck tie-breaking votes
for fuckers like Hegseth,
right-wing propagandists
posing as patriots.

Fuck your assault
on judicial independence.
Fuck ideological wars
against climate action
and democracy itself.

Fuck misogyny.
Fuck patriarchy.
Fuck white supremacy.
Fuck racism.
And fuck aligning
with the AfD.

Fuck your erasure
of trans, racialized, queer,
and immigrant lives
in art, in books, in public.

Fuck your bullshit in Greenland,
and your racist dismissal
of Chinese people
as "peasants"
in public remarks.

Fuck criminalizing
gender-affirming care.
Fuck stripping
nonbinary markers
from passports.

Fuck your refusal
to protect
same-sex marriage.

Fuck shaming IVF,
family planning, fertility options.
And fuck your obsession
with child-centric nationalism.

Fuck calling teachers
without children
"cat ladies"
and threats to families.

Fuck Project 2025,
taking over civil service.
Fuck backing extreme
executive power.

Fuck your policies
of mass deportation,
border walls,
and punishing
immigrants for
sending money home.

Fuck racist lies
about Haitian neighbors.
Fuck flirting with fascists,
and batting lashes at Russia.
Fuck justifying hatred
with nationalist religion.

Fuck repealing
environmental protections.

Fuck Vance!

Musk

Fuck Musk.
Nazi salute,
chats with Weidel,
affirming AfD,
fascist nostalgia,
Germany's
"last spark of hope."

Fuck xAI,
self-labeled
MechaHitler.

Fuck X,
white supremacy,
shelter for bigots.

Fuck DOGE,
open racism
with a paycheck.

Fuck mass layoffs,
calling Palestinian
education "hate school."

Fuck interference,
election meddling,
data harvesting,
dystopian
America Party.

Fuck
the ugliest cybertruck
on Earth.

And fuck every person
driving that boxy ass
Nazi-mobile.

Executive Orders

Fuck your EOs,
withdrawing from WHO,
renaming the Gulf,
attacking birthright citizenship,
ending asylum,
deporting millions
after torturing them.

Fuck "Remain in Mexico,"
restrictions on care,
calling it mutilation,
erasing nonbinary gender,
affirming transphobia,
binary lies,
denial of science.

Fuck cutting federal funds
for gender-affirming care.
Fuck criminalizing identity,
and trying to
remove us entirely.

Fuck criminalizing teachers
for affirming queer kids.
Fuck dismantling DEI,
stripping protections
from civil servants,
killing remote work.

Fuck ending climate protections.
Fuck affirming the death penalty,
weaponized against immigrants,

erasing narratives
of colonization, slavery,
racial justice.

Fuck attacking PBS.

Fascism

Crushing dissent
and descent through
silencing critics,
censorship, imprisonment,
exile, assassination.
Our words are dangerous.

Democracy eliminated,
institutions dismantled,
elections rigged,
courts disempowered,
corruption reigns when
laws are weaponized
against us.

Cults of personality
uphold leaders who
rape, kill, eliminate
human rights, preferably
all marginalized people.
Loyalty to him elevates
cult before humanity.

State-sanctioned violence
terrorizes masses with
police. Military state
brutalizes those of us
most vulnerable,
protestors, and anyone
with enough guts to
disagree.

Targets on our backs.
Those who are queer,
immigrant, disabled,

racialized, or who worship
differently or not at all.
We are the opponents,
scapegoats, dangerous
villains to attack.

Constant monitoring.
Phones, internet,
media, neighbors.
Someone is listening,
waiting for missteps
to threaten and control.
Fear rules the day.

Propaganda shits on truth,
lies shit on truth
until everyone believes
rewritten education,
news, and art
serving the regime,
not humanity.

History fades away,
erased and distorted.
Inconvenient truths buried.
Slavery, genocide,
colonialism, queer history.
Wouldn't want masses
recognizing how to
stop the hate and who
is ultimately responsible.

Weapons, war, and police
parade the streets,
civilian life simply preparing
for destruction to come.

Banning books,
art, music, ideas,
anything unpatriotic,
woke, degenerate.
(Code for truthful.
Code for diverse.)

Genocide
and ethnic cleansing
happen when "they"
stand in the way of "order,"
or contaminate "purity."
Mass murder.
Mass incarceration.
Mass hate.

Bodies are owned,
reproduction dictated,
autonomy disallowed
in favor of enforced birth,
sterilization, parenthood,
roles in society.

Nationalism forced
with flags, pledges,
slogans, "Make America
Great Again." What?
Like when slavery
normalized trafficking?
You fucking MAGATS.

Labor rights die,
Unions banned,
state controlled
alternatives
eliminate rights to

organize, strike,
negotiate, or even
seek safety.

Rigid gender roles
punish trans people,
subordinating women
to state and male rule.
White supremacy
overarching it all.

Artistic voices, poets
silenced, imprisoned,
exiled, murdered.
Mysteriously disappeared.
True expressions
vanishing entirely.

Religion is weaponized,
justifying violence,
exclusion, control.
Your hymns are nothing
more than justification
for state control.

Rigged systems ensure
accused people have
zero defense against
horrors that persist,
that their innocence
doesn't matter at all.

Economic inequality
protects the wealthy,
elite, billionaires.
Working class suffers
for their profit
and evil delight.

Fascism ends in blood,
yours and mine,
mass violence, war,
collapse, revolution,
destroying countless
sacred lives in the process.

Poverty

Poverty is politic,
not failure.

Poverty leverages
codes and laws
to trap you.

Poverty is never
low income.
Poverty is underpaid.

Poverty funds existence
for billionaires,
exploiting labor and
extracting from the poor.

Poverty is death
when healthcare is tied
to employment.

Poverty is bankruptcy
when GoFundMe fails
and cancer bills prevail.

Poverty lies about
personal responsibility,
when systems were rigged
all along. Intentionally.

Poverty is being unhoused
when evictions are a
literal fucking business model.

Poverty is starvation
and malnourishment
when food deserts are
manufactured by design.

Poverty is enforced
generationally.
Red lining. School funding.
Property tax. Inheritance laws.
Systemic racism.

Poverty rewards
corporate greed,
demonizing welfare.

Poverty is criminalized.
Can't pay a ticket?
Sleeping in your car?
Arrested.

Poverty brings stress,
pollution, untreated
chronic illness,
despair, and violence.

Poverty is unsafe
housing, hungry bellies,
underfunded schools,
and blame for not succeeding.

Poverty is trauma,
chronic stress, shame,
instability, survival mode,
and long-term risks.

Poverty is being judged
for using benefits
I paid taxes for,

treated like I'm stealing.

Poverty is punished,
is iron bars of impossibility,
community saving us,
at least sometimes.

Medicaid Cuts

Fuck your murderous
cutting of life,
someone's insulin,
cancer treatment,
ability to breathe.

Disabled, chronically ill,
elderly, children, pregnant,
poorest of the poor.
Blood is on your hands.

Fuck your death sentence,
your "fiscal responsibility,"
your ableism, every belief
that we are disposable.

Fuck dooming lives
to institutions so you
can have another yacht,
all while rural folx
are dying while trapped
in poverty.

Fuck your family destruction.
I thought you were pro-life,
but Jimmy's parents
lost jobs to keep him alive.

Fuck your white supremacy,
targeting Black and Brown bodies,
while criminalizing illness,
making emergency rooms
the only option to avoid death,
yet sometimes the door
to imprisonment.

Fuck your cruelty,
as mental health care
goes to the gutters, crisis
mounting without listening ears,
medications and safe spaces.

Fuck impossible choices,
pushing caregivers over the edge,
disappearing services,
closing hospitals,
and erasure of disabled rights.

Fuck killing people quietly
while looking smug,
never justifying your subsidies,
or admitting we deserve life.

Reflective Pause: Medicaid Cuts

Medicaid cuts eliminate access to lifesaving medications, treatments, and services that people rely on to survive. They declare that some lives are too expensive to save, exposing the ableist and eugenic logic that defines certain bodies as less worthy of care. For many, a deep, searing rage rises when care is denied simply because someone in power has decided certain people are not worth the cost.

That kind of systemic disregard is an assault on human rights. To live in a body that needs support and be told by lawmakers that your life is too expensive is a form of violence that is difficult to process. Our rage in response to this injustice screams, sobs, curses, and grieves. It bears witness as disabled people, chronically ill people, children, elders, caregivers, and entire communities are left to suffer or die in the name of "fiscal responsibility."

Reflective Writing

Have you or someone you love ever been denied care because of cost, insurance status, or access barriers? What did it feel like? How does it feel to name the connection between policy and pain, between budget cuts and lives lost? What does your anger want to say to the people making these decisions?

Food Stamp Cuts

We're so dehumanized
we don't even deserve
to eat.

Starving in the richest
nation on earth,
as if growling bellies
is personal failure.

Sure, punish sweet
innocent children,
this generational cruelty,
hitting disabled people
the very hardest.

Black and Brown folx
who built this country
starve as you clutch
your white supremacist
pearls with control
and work requirements.

Fuck stigmatizing survival,
making us undeserving,
while engineering
lack of access to food,
creating impossible choices,
then fueling despair.

Fuck your racism,
references to
"welfare queens."
"Moochers."
Fucking dog whistles
building and built

on shame.

Fuck your economic
destruction, death
sentences from
malnutrition,
when you've never proved
you're deserving of
piles and piles
of Teslas on yachts
on houses on BMW
beach vacations.

Fuck your hatred
for single parents,
your political theatre
when food is a human right,
your games created poverty,
then you punish us
for being poor.

Fuck you.

Job Searches

You are proudly
committed to diversity,
but my pronouns, body size,
and his skin color are
somehow a liability.

We're just too much,
not a cultural fit.
Because why?

Too queer,
too Black,
too disabled,
too outspoken.

Just not the right vibe.

(Not you.)

My lived experience
makes me unreliable
but you love Chad's
semester in France.

Fuck your expectation
that we're smiling
and grateful for scraps.
$15 an hour bullshit
with masters degrees
and 90-minute commute.
We should be thanking you.

Fuck cover letters
where you expect us
to show our subservience

and beg at the feet
of our very oppressor.

You want "diverse candidates,"
but never leadership.
Put me in your brochure,
but tell me to let Angela
speak first.

Fuck your bias,
the way you see laziness
when cancer was the cause,
when illness was the cause,
when caregiving was the cause.

Network, you say,
but these rooms?
Never built for me,
rather to exclude me,
intimidate me,
and make me go away.

Fuck downplaying truth.
Trans activism is now
community engagement.
My ass. Boy bye.

Overqualified, yet underpaid,
contract worker on Medicaid.
And then my trauma
becomes a marketing scheme.

Emotional labor,
invisible labor
while I spend
20 hours this week
educating you for no pay.
Exploitation.

I'm too political
for simply existing,
while their name
costs them the interview.

Be authentic, you say,
but not me. Only Becky.

Accommodations? I must
be difficult. Not to mention
I put my soul
into this application
only to be ghosted,

except those three times
I was in the final round
only for cishet white women
to get the job, while society
told me I was failing.

Anger Suppression

Fuck the day you told me
my anger was dangerous,
to smile through pain,
and that my anger
makes you uncomfortable.

Your comfort always mattered
more than my pain.

Fuck the ways you pathologize my rage.
Hysterical. Unstable. Overreacting.
So I learn my safety depends
on staying small.

I internalized shame for feeling.

Fuck the day I learned to apologize
for existing, needing, questioning,
pushing back, excelling, breathing.

I learned to disappear.

Fuck your punishment
for boundary setting.
How dare I make it difficult
to oppress me.

You weaponized my calmness
as proof I wasn't harmed.

Fuck your damn labels
of aggression when I was
simply confident. A leader.

I learned to be the bigger person.

Fuck the crumbs you threw
while expecting gratitude,
as I kept the peace in this
fucked up system.

You rewarded cishet white men
for showing more anger than me.

Fuck your tone policing
and the fear instilled of
losing everything
if I disagree.

I learned to repress, suppress, control it.

Fuck calling me too much,
unhinged or reactive.

You taught me to
caretake your emotions.

Fuck expressing anger sideways
without my full voice,
always educating,
never erupting.

I learned to be silent.

U.S. Concentration Camps

Call them processing centers,
but they are death camps.

Men housed next to alligators.
No escape, no humanity,
held for months, maybe years,
but no charges.

Guards mock them,
make them eat like dogs.
Racial slurs, threats,
comparisons to slave keepers.

Medical neglect,
deaths without insulin
or heart medication.
Covered up.

But the lights stay on,
night or day,
who can say,
then hunger strikes
land you in solitary.

Fuck your retaliation
against whistleblowers,
while detention is privatized,
evil actors profiting
from zero transparency.

Fuck separating children,
parents, siblings,
forcibly sterilizing people
or raping them to
bear children.

Fuck forced labor,
ignored outbreaks,
bullying queer detainees,
and deporting in
active appeals.

Fuck destroying documents,
racial profiling,
white supremacy,
and every dollar
of tax funds paying
for all of us to have
blood on our hands.

White Evangelical Christianity

You fucking worship
whiteness, not Jesus.
Use beliefs to
justify slavery,
weaponizing
family values,
attacking
queer families,
while hiding abuse
in your pews,
and pretending to be
pro-life, yet
celebrating war,
gun violence,
capital punishment,
and forced birth.

You fucking worship
capitalism, not Jesus.
Use prosperity gospel
to blame poor people,
calling billionaires blessed,
while supporting fascists
in exchange for power.
Trump. DeSantis. JD.

You fucking worship
cruelty, not Jesus,
erasing his teachings.
Cut food stamps,
not feed the hungry.
Build the wall,
not welcome the stranger.

You fucking worship
sexual abuse, not Jesus,
running purity culture
like a goddamn cult,
shaming girls,
blaming survivors,
worshipping virginity
more than consent.

You fucking worship
lies, not Jesus.
Pray harder.
God won't give you
more than you can bear.
You're out of alignment.
(All to maintain control.)

You fucking worship
oppression, not Jesus.
Submission for women,
children, Black folx,
queer folx, disabled folx,
anyone you want to control
with your fucked-up cross
in one hand, rifle in the other,
yet if you doubt, that's a sin.

You fucking worship
fear, not Jesus.
Wouldn't want empathy,
feelings, kindness,
or love to rain on
your parade of charades.

You fucking worship
bigotry, not Jesus.
Black theology,
Queer theology,

Latine theology
equals heresy,
excommunication.
White theology only.

You fucking worship
rapists, not Jesus.
Silencing survivors
with forgive and forget,
don't gossip, you're
ruining his ministry,
sowing division,
and thinking only of yourself.

You fucking worship
colonization, not Jesus.
Your white saviorism
tries to "save" people
but ignores genocide
voted in by you.

You fucking worship
whiteness, not Jesus.
Your damned "colorblind"
means you never,
ever, fucking never
admit to or address
your racism.

You fucking worship
complacency, not Jesus,
refusing to dismantle injustice,
while turning churches
into mega moneymaking
machines. Corporations first,
confusing empire for faith.

White Christian Nationalism

God and country.
One fucking idol
of a trinity comprised
of Jesus,
the U.S. Constitution
(when convenient),
and a blazing white man
with a gun.

Patriotism is obedience,
questioning the president
is heresy, dissent is sin.

Didn't you hear?
The United States
is God's chosen nation!
Fucking gag me.

Your Bible replaces
the constitution
with white supremacy,
patriarchy, and power.

Churchy political machines
summon pastors for
campaign rallies,
propagandists to the
fucking extreme.

Crosses and confederate flags,
Jesus justifying fascism,
and religious freedom,
but only for you
and the whole damn
redneck crew.

Forced birth
in Jesus' name.
Violence sanctified
in Jesus' name.
Indigenous erasure
in Jesus' name.
Queer genocide
in Jesus' name.

Start them young
with prayer in school,
patriotic education,
pledge of allegiance,
book bans,
and gender roles.

Call on the name of Jesus
to invoke racial hierarchy
where white is wondrous,
and everything else
is somehow unnatural,
impure, disgusting,
and dangerous.

Demonize democrazy
unless for your means,
abolishing separation
of church and state,
hailing cruel leaders,
rewriting history
with evil messiahs,
theocracy burning books,
shouting blasphemy!

Reflective Pause: White Christian Nationalism

White Christian Nationalism wraps violence in scripture, cloaks white supremacy in religious language, and weaponizes patriotism against the very people it claims to protect. It elevates obedience over justice, dominance over love, and purity over truth, disguising spiritual and emotional abuse as righteousness.

It is enraging to watch religion used as a justification for genocide, forced birth, queer erasure, transphobia, xenophobia, racist violence, and more. It is infuriating to witness a movement invoke Jesus as a cover for power, control, and cruelty, turning spiritual language into a weapon of domination and fear. This kind of manipulation thrives on silence, fear, and exhaustion.

Naming White Christian Nationalism as a violent, exclusionary force is an essential act of truth-telling and an expression of righteous anger. Rage is sacred when it exposes lies, confronts them, and helps clear a path toward justice. When you give your anger a voice, you help unravel the systems that depend on your silence.

Reflective Writing

Where have you seen religion used as a tool of domination or control? How did it make you feel? What would it look like to channel that anger into disruption, truth-telling, or community care?

Write what enrages you about White Christian Nationalism. Let it roar, shake the silence, and demand to be heard. Your anger is a welcome and vital part of the resistance.

War and Bombing

Fuck seeing children
as collateral damage,
precision bombing,
hitting hospitals, schools,
homes, playgrounds.

Fuck civilian deaths
sanitized as
surgical strikes,
neutralized targets
never named as
murdered families.

Fuck empire weapons
sold to both sides,
war branded as freedom,
and sending the poor
to die.

Fuck white phosphorous
and cluster bombs,
and the trauma that
doesn't end
when bombs do.

Fuck cultural erasure,
underfunded rebuilding,
war zones as testing grounds,
and make believing
it's all humanitarian.

You are fucking evil,
bombing weddings,
funerals, sacred places,
then televising it

to watch like sports.

Fuck your racist disdain
for the Global South,
your cruel creation
of generational grief,
fueling of fascism.

You treat refugees like threats,
turning away as mothers
scream for babies
over rubble,
ensuring there's always
money for bombs.

Palestine

Thousands of lives gone.
Gone.

You're debating
their humanity?

You offer
no food, water, safety?
Starve them.

Journalists exposing
hatred are silenced.

You ignore
families wiped from registries?

Gaza's poets, doctors,
teachers, bakers,
disappeared.

You believe
the Nakba ended?

Mothers, sisters, brothers,
cousins, friends, denied the right to mourn.

You embrace
conflating Zionism and Judaism?

We fund
the missiles and death warrants.

You think
conflict is more accurate than genocide?

Palestinian flags
are banned.

You want
more voices deplatformed?

Students are
surveilled.

You support
bombing UN shelters?

Everyone said never again.
But here we are, again.

You demand
we stop talking ceasefire?

You hate, yet they sing, resist,
dance Dabke on ruins.

Now, what about you?

Options

What fucking options?
Every door locked.
Job application discarded.
Landlord exploitive.
Mortgage company predatory.
Doctor bigoted.
Healthcare revoked.
Food inaccessible.
Mental health unsupported.

And hard work lands you
in a food desert,
a transportation desert,
disability later punishing
you for surviving.

What fucking options
for queer youth kicked out,
trans youth forced back,
libraries shuttered,
and "right to work"
means no rights at all.
Unprotected,
criminalized for existing,
then unhirable.

Fascism pushes you
into hiding for thinking.
Surveillance waits,
ready to catch you again
for what?
Surviving.

Certain others rise
while you're still drowning,

weights on your ankles.

They say
work on your mindset,
listen to the rich.

But this American Dream
was never
meant
for you.

Academia

Get your degree
and be successful.

Fuck you.

Gatekeeping dressed as rigor.
Whitewashed curricula.
Tuition debt before a salary.
Tenure for racists.
Adjuncts exploited.
Disability accommodations
that don't accommodate.

Tokenism.
DEI panels for show.
Inaccessible language.
Citations over lived experience.
"Objective" research
upholding empire.
Oppression disguised
as scholarship.

Professors stealing work.
No credit for racialized students.
Being the only ____ in the room.
Ethics boards
silencing the most ethical voices.

Burnout romanticized.
Rest framed as failure.
Mental health crisis,
covered up.

Conferences only
the wealthy attend.

We are studied
but never invested in.

Corrupt donors,
tainted endowments,
language policing,
and then—

"Too activist,"
for daring to say
anything at all.

Funding

Gutted:
Programs gone overnight.
Housing assistance.
2SLGBTQIA+ centers.
Mental health support.
Public school budgets.
SNAP benefits.
Arts and culture grants.
Black-led anything.
Indigenous-led anything.
Youth programs.
Legal aid.
Refugee support.
Immigrant support.
Disability services.
Any mention of diversity.
Climate change concerns.
Reproductive healthcare.
HIV services.
Veteran and elder care.
Trans healthcare.
Scholarships for the marginalized.
Everything nourishing,
liberating,
healing.

And then
every last ounce
of patience I had
for every single
one of you who
voted this bullshit
into office.

FUCK YOU.

Anti-DEI

Anti-DEI = anti-me.
Probably anti-you.

Dismantled mandates.
Lost my contracts.
Stripped protections.

So, you must certify,
attest, state clearly
you never, ever,
not even a little,
run DEI programs.

Fuck your layoffs,
cancelled contracts,
removed resources,
and archived
equity plans.

Fuck removing
representation,
websites, histories,
people, jobs,
positions, futures,
dreams, histories.

Fuck purging
DEI language,
scrutinizing programs,
cancelled grants,
canning school programs
teaching children
we all belong
and are welcome here.

Fuck patriotic campuses,
demonizing pro-Palestinian
demonstrations,
and frozen funds for schools
unwilling to comply.

Fuck disrupting
VA trans healthcare,
corporations being
chicken shit, rolling back
initiatives.

Well, watch us
roll our wallets
the fuck up, too.

Fuck DEI watch lists.
Yes, I've seen my name.

I've seen the injunctions,
the challenges, and
my existence proving
no matter how hard
you try to eliminate us,

We. Are. Still. Here.
to spite you.

Anger at You?

Fucking pissed
at *you*,
because well,
can't you pull it together?
I mean seriously,
get it the fuck together!

Or wait.

Fucking pissed that *you*
reminded me of
everything else
under the sun that is
not okay,
which is why you can't
just pull it together.

You burst my bubble,
my illusion of okay-ness,
of pretty days and rainbows,
with reality's hammer
crashing the fuck into
the beginning of my day.

You're not okay
because it's not okay,
and if it's not okay,
then I'm not okay,
and I am grief stricken
for every way the system
is crushing us.

Fucking pissed it's not
your fault or my fault,

we can't fix it today.
Fuck it. Fuck you.
Fuck me.
Fuck every bit of it.

Big UGLY Bill

Fuck you every day,
as you smile, cheer,
snicker and sneer,
while folx shout,
beg and plea:
"STOP hurting us!
People will DIE!"

Fuck you every day
my family starves
from SNAP cuts,
after cancer
rained on our
income parade.
Pantries closed,
cupboards bare,
and we'd rather die
than live like this.
But we refuse
to beat you
to the grave.

Fuck you every day,
when Medicaid cuts
cause my children
to one day live
without me,
as I die without
lifesaving meds,
doctor's visits
I can't fucking make.

Fuck you every day
people live in fear
of masked men

disappearing them
into camps,
never to see
or hug
their babies again.

Fuck every person
who voted for this bill,
this genocide,
this military state,
these politicians,
who justified it
over egg prices,
billionaire tax breaks,
and lies,
thin disguises
for your fucking hatred,
even in your own eyes.

Fuck you every day!
May the hate you hold
haunt you 1,000 times.
May fire ants
invade your ass,
never stop biting,
the itch flooding
your every thought
until you can never
hurt or kill
anyone again!

FUCK THE 4TH

FUCK THE 4TH,
THE FIREWORKS,
AND THE HATE.
FUCK EMPIRE.
FUCK COLOIZERS.
FUCK THE WHOLE
HOUSE OF HORRORS.
FUCK MASKED MEN
BEATING, TORTURING
DISAPPEARING BELOVEDS.
FUCK BLOODY RED,
AND THE BLUE
WAVING FLAGS,
AND ESPECIALLY
THE FUCKING WHITE
WHO AIN'T NEVER
BEEN RIGHT.

CONNECT

Harnessing Collective Anger for Social Change

"We are not only fighting for our lives, but we are also fighting for our joy, our pleasure, our right to be seen and heard."

— PATRISSE CULLORS, *WHEN THEY CALL YOU A TERRORIST*

Ponderings on Connecting Through Anger

Anger has the power to connect us. One of its most overlooked gifts lies in its potential to draw us into deeper relationships with others. While anger often begins as a personal sensation rising in our own bodies, it can also become a force that moves us toward collective healing, shared empowerment, and meaningful social transformation.

Too often, we are taught to keep our anger quiet and to relate to it as something shameful or dangerous. We are told to manage it alone; to suppress it so it does not inconvenience others or disrupt the status quo. But what if our anger is not the problem? What if the real issue is the way we are told to carry it in silence, and then hold it in isolation, disconnected from the communities and systems that could help hold, respond to, and transform it?

When anger is given space to be witnessed and shared, it demonstrates its capacity to galvanize movements, bring people together, and carve out space for new systems rooted in justice. Expressing our rage in community has the potential to validate our experiences, remind us we are not alone, and help us remember that we are part of something larger than ourselves. In this way, anger knits together our collective struggle, healing, and power.

Through the pages ahead, we explore how anger becomes a tool of connection. From art that speaks truth to power, to grassroots organizing that builds new futures, to protests that echo the voices of the unheard, we see how anger unites us in action. These expressions dismantle the structures that harm us while also nurturing the emergence of more equitable ways of relating. Anger helps us see what is broken, and it also helps us imagine what could be built in its place.

The poems in this section speak to that duality, honoring the full-bodied reality of rage and the urgency it brings while celebrating the connections it forges between people, as well as across movements and time. They remember the anger of our ancestors and uplift the vision of future generations. They remind us that when we fight together, we do so not only out of pain, but also out of love for other people, our planet, and the affirming equity we believe is possible.

The work of processing our anger in community is at once deeply spiritual and deeply practical. It is found in protests, resistance rituals, healing spaces, policy writing, and the construction of mutual aid networks. It is visible through teach-ins, storytelling, and communal sharing of complex truths. Whether through song, poetry, panels, or grassroots mobilization, anger helps us break silences, disrupt gaslighting, and center the needs of those most impacted.

Our anger does not make us broken. It makes us aware, alerts us to injustice, and compels us to act. It is our fire. When we recognize its wisdom and catalyze it through our communities, it becomes a force that resists the systems that oppress us and the internalized stories that tell us we are not allowed to feel or fight back.

Let this section remind you that your anger is part of something bigger than yourself. It also belongs to the generations who came before you and those who will come after. It can live in community, where it is witnessed, honored, and used to create something powerful and good. In a world that tries to divide and isolate us, choosing to connect through our anger is a radical act of love, hope, and possibility.

Publications

Our anger funnels
righteously and rightfully
into that op-ed,
the university zine
opening minds to
realities unseen.

Consider rageful exposés,
political poetry anthologies,
marginalized magazines
amplifying underrepresented
hostility toward hate.

Collaborative books,
memoirs of resistance,
radical manifestos,
and decolonial journals
blasting white supremacist
ideals into fires of
heartfully lived experience.

Graphic novels and comics
for the kids, unsent letters,
oral history projects,
intersectional publishing
houses daring to amplify
what everyone else
tries to deny.

Satire and humor,
publishing scholars
intent on unsettling
every arm of empire
with books on
mutual aid, grassroots

organizing, boasting
educational toolkits
to equip them young.

Self-published works
subvert prescribed orders,
every work dangerous
to prescribed systems
thriving when intellect
is cold and dead.

Protest Art

City wall murals
demand justice,
not hate.

Posters,
street installations,
and graffiti tags
surrounding silence
with truth until
roars of justice
applaud fearlessness.

Chalk art,
political cartoons,
giant puppets,
and photography
offers representations
where uprisings,
brutality and resistance
need amplification.

Projection art
makes the elite fart,
while art therapy
turns their gas
into powerful forces
for flying.

Protest shirts,
sculptures from debris,
interactive installations
where everyone is finally
free to scream,
releasing tension
to ascension for our

higher good.

Digital art,
then tattoo art,
banners,
coloring books
and painting circles.

Our rage creates
beauty
where hate
fought for silence.

Storytelling

I'll tell my grandchildren,
and they will tell me.

So will our circle,
over knitting needles,
quietly sipping tea.

You'll shout on corners
as they record podcasts.

Memorial services
where grief is held with care.

Story quilts.
History tours.
Documentaries.
Sacred monologues.

What if we rap with kids
after school,
subverting propaganda
with their words in murals?

Anonymous letters,
radio dramas,
book readings,

or you and me,
simply meeting
here to listen
and share.

Music and Theatre

Protest choirs
with rewritten verses,
belted freely.
Flash dance.

Ancestral fire
channeled in rhythm,
drum circles for
social change.

Guerrilla theatre,
punk bands,
surprise performances,
queer fury
cabarets.

Hip hop cyphers,
drag performers,
rage operas,
interactive plays.

Theatre of the Oppressed,
concerts for mutual aid,
protest songs rallying

for decolonizing forces,
agitators interested in
underground dismantling
of every system of harm.

Loudly.

Circles and Rituals

Our hearts open space
where broken glass,
burnt matches,
and protest flyers

invite our rage into safety,
collective screams
meeting the sky,
like our pens to paper.

Candles bear stories,
voices disclosing harms
no longer held
in blood and bones alone.

Sticks and stones
encircle our hands,
as poetry circles with
this one shared object,
symbolically shredding,

leading the way
to circles of protest,
our creative rituals
washing shame away,
voicing what we refuse,

rage songs burning
hatred, protest messages
building from person
to person to person,
our naming ritual
leaving us connected

for all that is to come.

Social Media

Masked men appear,
livestreams exposing
their evil for gestapo.

The viral carousel
exposes realities
banned from news,
when propaganda tries
to hold the last word.

Hashtag campaigns
and amplified voices,
comment floods,
and fact-checking missions.

Voice notes and reels
organize block-outs,
anonymous voicing rage,
sharable content
getting the word out.

Rage relays,
then grief to anger
processing sessions,
youth led anger
showcasing stories
systematically.

Policy documents
expose corruption,
and a day in my life
showcases rage,
followed by our
complete digital
protest. Strike.

Grassroots Movements

What do you mean
when you say
things will
never change?

Try
door-to-door listening,
teach-ins,
communal empowerment,
mutual aid pods,
one big assembly,
rage clinics,
political education days,
coalition tables,
angry zines,
flyer drop-offs,
occupying spaces,
strike funds,
hardship funds,
accountability collectives,
neighborhood leaders,
visioning sessions,
protest kitchens,
running for office,
self-defense class,
disrupting meetings,
direct action,
archives of struggle
and success.

Just try,
let your anger
refuse regret.

Protest

Die-ins.
Silent marches.
Rolling blockades.
Flash mobs.

Would you protest
like that?

Street theatre.
Mass arrests.
Banner drops.
Noise protests.

How about like that?

Encampments.
Sit-ins.
Torchlight vigils
rising into rallies.

Could you show up,
with anger,
with rage,
for that?

Speech interruptions.
Youth walkouts.
Anniversary marches.
Coordinated disruption.

When should we
meet face to face?

Bridge takeovers.
Demonstrations

at trauma sites.
Financial blackouts.
General strikes.

How else
might you dare
to fight?

Mutual Aid

When life feels
impossible,
injustice squashes hope,
but anger creates—

emergency housing,
community bail funds,
medical supply closets,
childcare co-ops,
nonprofit therapy,
survival funds grown with care,
free dinner programs,
ACAB neighborhood watch,
protest first-aid,
barter networks,
mobile resource vans,
seed exchanges,
community gardens,
ride shares,
home repair crews,
skill-swap collectives,
specialty workshops,
food pantries,
free stores,
neighborhood fridges,
moving crews,
free clinics,
debt relief,
memorial support,
closets for workwear.

Anger becomes beauty,
connection rooted in love.

Reflective Pause: Mutual Aid

When systems fail us, mutual aid grows from the soil of anger, love, and the refusal to leave each other behind. Mutual aid says, "We keep us safe." It takes the rage of injustice and transforms it into connection, care, and survival.

These networks exist because people got angry enough to create what the system refused to provide. We see mutual aid at work through the free fridge on the corner, a neighborhood watch that does not call the cops, or a community medical fund. Childcare, meals, housing, transportation, community gardens, and tool libraries are also rooted in the belief that we are not disposable and that another way is possible.

Reflective Writing

What forms of mutual aid have you received, witnessed, or participated in? How did it feel? Where do you see anger turning into care in your community? When you think about what you or your people have lacked, what do you long to create?

Write about a moment when collective care made you feel seen, held, or valued. Let your anger shape your vision for what we might build together.

Policy and Advocacy

Harm reduction
calms nonsense
as we burn
it all down,
building
something new.

Lobby days,
community-penned
legislation,
policy scorecards.

Testimony.
Public hearings.
Model drafting.
Bill tracking
for all to see.

Coalitions formed.
Movements aligned.
Ballot initiatives.
Demands to
divest from ICE.

Co-governance.
Amicus briefs.
Shadow town halls.
Whistleblower
protections.
Deplatforming
lobbyists who
prioritize profit
over people.

Community safety.
Human rights
resolutions rising.

Civil Disobedience

Yes, you can.
Consequences? Yes.
Worth it? You decide.

Refusing to pay.
Occupying offices.
Interrupting
shareholder meetings.
Confronting exploitation
they'd rather fund
than expose.

Breaking curfews.
Sleeping where you
damn well please.
Chalking slogans
on every surface.

Sitting firmly
where you're unwanted.
Teaching in spaces
of corruption
and transportation.

Blocking traffic.
Breaking dress codes.
Disrupting legislative sessions
with chants of
rageful love.

Removing signs.
Covering lies
with truth-telling messages
of collective resistance.

Nonviolent trespass.
Leaking documents.
Sharing evidence.
Hosting banned
drag shows and
pride events.

Burning contracts,
eviction notices,
certain flags.
Refusing to work.
Calling a sick out.

Using banned words.
Speaking with fire.
Language, freely.
Public funerals.
Mock trials.
Turning off tracking.

And knowing nothing.
Seeing nothing.
No one spoke.

Community Safety

Neighborhood patrols
that look like you,
eyes on pig brutality.

De-escalation.
Conflict resolution.
Free self-defense classes
for folx targeted by hate.

Phone trees.
Rapid response networks.
Ready to mobilize support.
Offering sanctuary
and shelter.

Equip trans kids
with everything needed,
for navigating schools
and homes
that would rather
see them dead.

Firearm safety classes.
Legal rights workshops.
Street medic training.
Voter watch systems.
Encrypted communication,
always.

Safe walks.
Safe rides.
Eyes on hate groups.
Open-source intelligence.
Mutual alert systems.
Surveil hate.

Digital self-defense
against doxxing,
harassment,
cyberstalking.
We keep us safe.

Harm reduction kits.
Drug safety stations.
Local response hubs
with water, meds,
supplies, and tools
for self-defense.

Youth mentoring clubs.
Volunteer training.
Bystander intervention.
Shared protocols
to protect against
state actors.

Reclaiming land.
Reclaiming public space
for gatherings,
ceremonies,
shelter,
community care.

Cross-racial.
Interfaith.
Solidarity defense coalitions.
Preventing scapegoating,
violence,
and hate.

Teach and Learn

Expose bullshit,
breaking down
policy, history,
and power.

Understand it
to dismantle it.

Open rage rooms
for community
expression of anger
while learning
where it comes from.

Intergenerational
knowledge exchange,
where all ages
resist together,

knowing wisdom
defies age.

Propaganda
identification
education.
Red flags
of disinformation

signal opportunities
to see clearly now.

Know your rights,
legal workshops,
protest safety,
organizing,

and resistance
communication
protocols

that keep us united,
safe and connected.

Healing justice,
trauma education,
processing spaces,
tools for transforming
anger to action

so we don't embolden
hatred with niceties.

Panels amplifying
marginalized voices,
political education
sessions on injustice,
settler colonialism,
capitalism,
white supremacy

so we don't internalize
oppression as shame.

Leader training programs,
mock scenarios
of civil disobedience,
sessions exposing the cost
of silence, neutrality,
performative allyship

so accountability
keeps us moving forward.

Lived experiences
trump credentials.
Grassroots wisdom
blooms in workshops
mapping local
power structures,

creating opportunities
to strategically disrupt them.

Global organizers
and scholars share
how they disrupt,
fostering solidarity

where we remember
our liberation is connected.

Emotional literacy
and somatic tools
support harnessing
every ounce of anger
constructively

so we disrupt systems
instead of self-destruct.

Media analysis
uncovers
representation
gaps, strategic
roles in perpetuating
injustice, hate
and harm for
profit

so we co-create spaces
where none of us are experts,
but every person is accountable.

Facilitating Conversations

Brave space agreements
name power, boldly
inviting conflict
transformation,
normalizing anger
as sacred.

Story circles
open shared rage
where loneliness
is snuffed out
in emotional validation.
I see you. Me too.

Speak from your wound,
tell me what keeps you
awake at night
when social media
shows us both active
instead of resting.

Fishbowl discussions
necessarily amplify
marginalized voices
first, more privileged
people listening
silently.

Somatic anchoring
invites noticing
anger's residence
in our bodies
neutrally, without
pathologizing
or casting out.

Power-sharing
facilitation
crosses identity
lines, modeling
equity, affirmation,
and accountability.

Stop
tone policing
in real time.
Right now.
That shit is
pure violence.

Your poem
is a conversation
starter, and have you
seen their zine?
Raw emotion
and truth spark
dialogue.
Connection.

Debriefing spaces
following protest
ensure we express
not repress,
process fury,
build strategy,
and move.

Facilitated silence,
pauses between
breaths, then
breaths taken together,
disrupt the
urgency culture
of white supremacy.

Rotated facilitation roles,
consent-based conversation,
checking on capacity
before diving into trauma.

Rage mapping
opens awareness to
shared anger sources,
collective pain
and trauma
for processing
and action.

Cross-movement
dialogue spaces
intentionally connect
our causes and pain,
offering intersectional
views of radical
solidarity.

Call-in sessions,
call-out sessions,
abolitionist circles,
and facilitated
grief-to-action
transitions center
anti-gaslighting
dialogues where
we see what is real,
validating rage
in protest of
minimization.

Disrupting Narratives

You know damn well
the joke isn't funny,
so don't laugh.

Fucking correct
false narratives
like slavery
or ICE
as necessary evils.

Dare to ask
who benefits
from this version
of the story
in classrooms,
boardrooms,
or living rooms.

Name
spiritual bypassing
instead of
letting it slide,
in favor of
gratitude,
anesthetizing
the masses
into inaction.

Be truthful
with children
about race,
gender,
war, poverty
and empire.

Design alternative
family trees
honoring
chosen family,
queer lineage,
trans lineage,
_____ lineage.
Honor the ancestors.

Interrupt narratives
of "we're family"
at work, prompting
honest conversations
about power,
labor and equity.

Refuse to shrink
or hide identities
for anyone
or in any space,
simply for the sake
of respectability
politics and upholding
harmful systems
and hate.

Narrate your own
story, claim it
as your own,
disallowing anyone
to define your worth
for you.

Tell them to
fuck off.
Refuse participation
in conversations

debating your
humanity in
churches,
schools,
or homes.

Start a group chat
questioning
everything shady
happening at work,
daring to question
leadership, dismantle
systems, and
seek equity.

Stop romanticizing
the "good old days,"
trying to move backward
instead of seeking
forward momentum.

Queer the holidays,
start new traditions,
invite different people,
center voices
often silenced.

Use your voice
creatively,
to teach,
paint, write,
refusing to
celebrate
harmful observances.

Make your anger
visible and bold,

instead of hiding
behind false notions
and illusions of peace.

Reflective Pause: Disrupting Narratives

If you see something, say something. The lies of injustice are sometimes loud, but often they are quiet, spoken in code, passed off as jokes, wrapped in tradition, or disguised as family values. No matter how they show up, harmful narratives keep systems of oppression intact. Disrupting them takes clarity, courage, and a deep well of anger that says, "This isn't right, and I won't stay silent."

From classrooms to living rooms, workplaces to places of worship, dominant narratives are built to protect power and preserve the status quo. They sanitize history, romanticize oppression, and gaslight people into submission. Disruption doesn't have to be dramatic to be powerful. Sometimes it looks like starting a conversation. Other times it means not laughing along, or saying, "That's not true," even when your voice shakes.

Telling the truth is not always easy, but it is necessary. Your anger has the power to point you toward what needs to be questioned, challenged, and reimagined.

Reflective Writing

Where have you felt pressure to stay quiet when something harmful was said or done? What narratives have you internalized that no longer serve you or your communities? When have you disrupted a harmful story? What happened? What did it feel like?

Write about a time when anger pushed you to speak up or tell the truth. Let that moment guide you as you imagine new ways of moving forward.

Center the Most Marginalized

Promote leadership
represented by
those most impacted
by injustice,
carving narratives,
vision, and strategy
that work for all.

Accessibility first
for meetings, events,
and everyday work,
intentionally celebrating
each and everyone.

Pay people
instead of asking
for volunteers,
especially consultants
offering labor,
time, and precious
lived experience.

Child care,
transportation,
food,
and translation
ought to be
standard practice
everywhere.

Listen here.
Who is most harmed
by this system,
and how can we
follow their lead

instead of our own?

Protect racialized
trans femmes,
undocumented folx,
disabled folx,
and everyone else
most targeted.

Sliding scale models
are only equitable
when zero is an option.
So find funding
or don't offer the
workshop, service,
or "opportunity."

Refuse partnerships
with organizations
platforming hate,
no matter what,
and especially when
it costs you something
(or everything).

Feedback systems
are only effective when
marginalized members
have real power,
not just that one
trans kid,
the Brown man
in accounting,
or the student
in a wheelchair.
Do not tokenize.

Performative diversity
is the fucking devil,
so stop that shit,
and institute systems
and structures
designed for all
instead, even if
it takes longer
and costs more.

Embrace
transformative
justice,
instead of
leaning in
to carceral
(dis)logic.

Center marginalized
voices in every
publication,
podcast,
sermon,
and classroom,
without
tone policing
or relegating them
to special holidays
or months.

Disability justice
values are vital.
So rest, seek
interdependence,
slowness, and
community breath.

Multilingual
is the bare minimum.
How about
culturally rooted,
culturally responsive,
and co-created instead?

Platform redirecting
attention to anyone
silenced or erased,
even when brand
might feel off,
or you fear
retaliation.

Quit saviorism.
It's bullshit.
Quite collaborating
with white orgs
without accountability
to racialized leadership.

Willingly release
power, resources,
and prestige
in order to follow
Black, trans,
disabled,
Indigenous,
or intersectionally
marginalized leadership.

Name who is missing
in every room
and situation,

changing the room
until they are
both present
and safe.

Combat Gaslighting

Get receipts.
Document in real time,
preferably
with witnesses.

Journals.
Voice memos.
Messages with friends.

Validate memory
and perception.

Name gaslighting
for what it is.
Affirming practices
support your truth.

Create anything
that validates truth
for yourself
and others:

Zines.
Blog posts.
Social posts.
Videos.
Poems.
Art.
Books.
Literally anything.

Communally debrief.
Check in on friends.
Ask how they're
coping after harm.

They might feel alone,
and you will be the reason
they trust themselves.

Teach children
to name emotions
and set boundaries.
They will trust themselves.

Reject civility
that demands your silence,
compliance,
and the comfort
of harm-doers.

Support trauma-informed
journalism that centers
survivor voices
without retraumatizing
or doubting their truth.

Interrupt false binaries.
Good victim vs. bad victim,
real harm vs. imagined harm.

Believe survivors.
Rituals of truth-telling
create spaces
for believing,
caring,
affirming.

Refuse debates
that question
a human being's
right to exist.
Including your own.
That is not a debate.

Call out institutional gaslighting
in therapy,
medicine,
law enforcement,
education,
and religious messaging.

Seek media literacy.
Learn to dissect
dog whistles,
disinformation,
and other lies
in political
and religious messaging.

Honor your body's wisdom.
Listen when it says
something is off.
Believe its messages
more than others' words.

Use grounding,
tapping,
and sensory reminders
to anchor your truth.

"I believe you."
Sharing pain is courageous.
Support and care,
even if you
do not yet
fully understand.

Interrupt toxic positivity
and spiritual bypassing.
Speak the hard truth,
again and again.

Use language
that clearly reflects
your intent.
Repeat it.

Disrupt narratives
that frame
marginalized folx
as dramatic,
irrational,
or out of control.

Create archives
of memory and resistance.
Ensure against erasure.

Cooperatives and Collectives

Anger reimagines
economic systems,
visioning
anti-capitalist
models honoring
care, equity,
and liberation.

Transform intergenerational
trauma into leadership
through mentorship
within collectives.

Shared survival
infrastructures
create hope,
and channels
for survival in
housing,
food co-ops,
and sovereignty.

Oppose gentrification
with land trusts,
property collectives,
and efforts holding
heartfully to roots.

Fuck burnout culture.
Center rest, care,
and mutuality
in everything.

Health and wellness
collectives with

community providers
make healthcare
accessible to all.

Co-op jobs
subvert the prison
industrial complex,
reentry pathways
offering options
for thriving.

Healing centered
governance seeks
wholeness without
carceral logic,
democratic tools
decentering
white supremacist
leadership and
structures.

Equitable wealth
distribution and
redistribution
center marginalized
laborers, while
disrupting exploitative
practices and systems.

Timebanks
and barter systems
challenge harmful norms,
opening space for
creative collectives
to elevate voices
challenging dominant
narratives.

THE FORGOTTEN GIRLS

In a world where every crime tells a story, some voices remain eerily silent. In *The Forgotten Girls*, Dr. Alyce Clark, a passionate investigator and scholar, invites you to uncover the chilling realities behind the cold cases of women whose lives were cut short, yet whose stories have been overshadowed by time and society.

This gripping exploration delves into the lives of these women, revealing their dreams, struggles, and the profound impact of their untimely deaths on their families and communities. With meticulous research and heartfelt storytelling, Dr. Clark sheds light on the complexities of these cases, presenting not only the factual details but also the emotional truths that lie beneath the surface.

Join Dr. Clark on a journey through the shadows of crime and memory, where each chapter unveils the untold tales of resilience and tragedy. Discover the social realities that rendered these cases cold and learn why it is crucial to remember the forgotten.

Please help bring their stories back to light.

Dr. Alyce Clark is a retired Norfolk Police Detective, a veteran of the Army National Guard, and Keiser University's Forensic Department Chair. Her expertise in violent crimes and forensic investigations fuels her research on cold cases, the bystander effect, and critical incident stress. *The Forgotten Girls* is her first book.

TRUE
CRIME

WILDBLUE
P R E S S
wildbluepress.com

ISBN 978-1-964730-91-2

90000

9 781964 730912

Radical publishing
refuses to follow
oppressive rules
and demands,
in favor of amplifying
voices most needed
in this moment.

Coalitions of collectives,
sustainability co-ops,
accessibility focused
intentions, and rejection
of all hero-centered models
opens doors to
collective wisdom,
shared power,
equitable decisions,
and a more affirming
world for all.

New Spaces

Envision rage as sacred.
Challenge everything
pathologizing
or demonizing it.

Welcome emotional expression
openly, grief and rage
celebrated at the table.

Create circles centered
on grief and rage
due to systemic harm,
and let it all out
together.

Choose spiritual
community and practices
that expose religion's
complicity in
colonization,
racism,
and misogyny.

Create educational
spaces rooted
in consent
and bodily autonomy
for all people,
no matter what.

No.
Matter.
What.

Organize anger literacy
workshops,
support groups
challenging suppression,
offering expression,
and opportunities
to act together.

Liberatory theology
or deconstruction efforts
empower freedom
of thought, and
opportunities to
burn it all down,
then build it all up.

Community rooted
healing centers
offer third spaces
to rest, connect,
learn, and recover
from life under
siege of system.

Interfaith gatherings,
somatic education,
rituals deconstructing
systems of harm,
political workshops,
and spaces designed
to hold space
for righteous anger.

Offer opportunities
to understand rage
as a signal of harm,
boundaries violated,
call for protection,
reclamation, healing,
and collective action.

Alternatives to Policing

What if policing
is not the way to safety?

Envision
community-led
crisis response teams,
mobile mental healthcare,
conflict transformation collectives,

Street medics,
safety teams,
abolitionist training,
community mutual aid,
neighborhood care teams,
violence interruption programs.

Domestic violence
rapid response teams,
created to reduce risk.

Youth empowerment
teaching systems literacy,
self-advocacy,
and healing-centered safety.

Copwatch groups,
decarceral emergency lines,
community accountability circles,
neighborhood mutual defense groups.

Restorative justice hubs,
transformative justice pods,
decriminalization campaigns,
community safe homes and shelters.

Transformative justice collabs,
land-based sanctuary networks,
collective safety planning,
people's tribunals,
and truth commissions
exposing systems of violence,
elevating survivor stories,
seeking community-defined
justice over punishment.

Accountability and healing,
not policing.

Spirituality

Create meaning
birthed from resistance.

Liberation chants,
resistance poems,
call-and-response,
collective lament.

Rewriting texts,
truth-telling rituals,
resistance readings,
altered liturgies.

Protest songs,
sacred burning,
marking every soul
with symbols of
solidarity.

Community blessings,
memorial rituals,
intergenerational pledges
to protect children
from injustice.

Read banned books,
creating new rituals
affirming grief
and rage
through stones,
prayer cards,
protest relics,
and stories of
resistance.

Let this moment
of silence
and that change
center dignity,
and spiritual grounding
more than risk.

Ancestor Practice

Name the ancestors,
transcestors,
queercestors,
chosen family-cestors,
all the ancestors.

Share stories of
resistance, rage,
brilliance,
and survival,
gathering in twos,
or spread around
circles and fires
in the night.

Build altars
to collective
lineages of
justice seekers,
revolutionaries,
and truth-tellers,

knowing they would
want to hear from you,
so write them.
Letters asking for
strength, wisdom,
and presence.

Research and uncover
suppressed histories,
erased truths,
shouting realities
with pride to all
whose hearts listen.

Call the ancestors
to witness in vigils,
protests, and meetings,
affirming righteous
anger and powerful
movements for
resistance.

Invoke the ancestors
boldly for strength,
protection,
and guidance in
this moment.
They navigated
even worse.

Carry names
or objects in
your pockets,
your phone,
tattooed on
your skin,
knowing you
can always
connect with them.

Break generational
cycles of silence
to honor progress
and accountability
in continuing
the struggle.

Name the demons,
those colonizers,
abusers, harm-doers,
in commitment
to community justice

and ancestors wishing
us all good.

Vision and dream,
channeling fury
into creative
resistance,
reciting names
publicly, reclaiming
circles of care
in remembering.

Boundaried Resting

Fuck off.
Sometimes enough
is enough.

Turn off
the fucking news,
just for today.
Refuse unpaid
emotional labor
every fucking day.

Rotate caregiving
to ensure space
for everyone to rest.

Do not fucking disturb.
See this candle,
hear that music,
observe this affirmation?
My rest is ceremonial
and protected.

Block.
Breathe.
Rejoice.
No more shit,
no more exploitation,
no more intrusive
communications
without my consent.

Rest spaces.
Nap spaces.
Pleasure is necessary.
Bubble baths,

dance breaks,
orgasms,
random serenades,
and direct contradictions
to everything
wishing me miserable
or gone.
Fuck that.

Out of the office
for my fucking
mental health day.

These hours are mine.
Do not—
I repeat—
DO NOT
ask a damn thing
of me today.

Pause.
Breathe.
Delight and enjoy
to spite them,
but also to love me.

Thou shalt
honor my boundaries.
I shall also honor yours.

Fuck urgency culture.
I don't remember agreeing
to exhaust myself
with rushing.
My slowness
is resistance.

Celebrate my rest.

I want to celebrate your nap,
the video game savored
on an extra-long lunch,
and the candlelight dinners
we both enjoyed last night.

From here on out...

I am only saying yes
to what lights me up.
I refuse to center
oppressor comfort
in systems designed
for their benefit.

I do not exist
for your comfort.

I exist for me.
I shall live my life
and rest.

Watch.
Learn.
Repeat.

(Really. Go rest.)

Reflective Pause: Boundaried Resting

Boundaries carve out space to breathe, recover, and exist on your own terms. In a capitalist and white supremacist society that glorifies overextension and urgency, they are essential for survival. Anger helps us recognize when something has crossed the line and gives us the fire we need to protect our space, softness, and right to rest.

When we log off, silence our phones, or close our doors, we're reclaiming our right to choose how we engage with the world and when we pause. Staying informed matters, especially as fascism rises, but constant exposure without rest is unsustainable. Setting limits is one way we refuse to be constantly available for exploitation. It is a declaration that we deserve pleasure, stillness, and softness, simply because we are human.

Rest can take many forms. Sometimes it looks like a bath, a nap, or a dance break. Other times it's a walk in the park, a favorite game, or a long, quiet moment with someone who expects nothing from you. Rest might be solitude, or it might be community. However it shows up, let your body, your heart, and your needs guide how you use that space. It belongs to you.

Reflective Writing

What stops you from resting when you need it? Where in your life could anger help you set a boundary around your time, energy, or presence? What would it look like to protect your rest as something sacred and non-negotiable?

Write a permission slip for yourself to rest. Let your anger clear space for joy, for quiet, and for being.

Anger Says…

I matter.
You matter.
We matter.

Anger names harms,
resists erasure,
and interrupts
cycles of abuse,
even when everything
gets shaken up.

Anger prompts truth
to leak everywhere,
exploding into
the atmosphere,
walking out of rooms
gaslighting you.

Anger holds grief
tenderly, openly,
refusing to
accommodate
even an ounce
of oppression.

Anger demands repair,
changed behavior,
new systems and ways
of being together in
mutuality.

Anger says *hell no*!
I think the fuck not!
Fuck off!

Anger reveals aliveness,
keeping memory alive,
while forming alliances,
and confronting justice
daily.

Anger disrupts gaslighting,
bypassing, and suppression,
reclaiming narratives,
birthing boundaries,
and becoming sacred fire,
illuminating paths forward
when every fucking thing
tries to dim our light
into nothingness.

Anger stays alive!

Conclusion

Anger changes things. It interrupts silence, exposes injustice, and gives us our breath back. It is a force for change that rises within us to say enough is enough. Through these pages, I hope your anger has felt seen, heard, and honored.

We began with an invitation to rethink everything we were taught about anger. Together, we peeled back layers of suppression, named the systems that taught us to disconnect from our rage, and took an honest look at the cost of staying silent. We excavated the anger we carry in our bodies, naming the ways it whispers, screams, hides, and persists. We explored the complexity and nuance of anger in all its forms, including resentment, devastation, irritation, and fury. We found ways to express anger through movement, creativity, voice, and action. Finally, we imagined how anger might help us build new ways of being, rooted in equity, community, and care.

As we close this journey together, I want to pause and offer one final reflection, grounded in everything we have uncovered. One of the lesser-known gifts of anger is that it often opens the door to deeper healing. For many of us, anger creates safety. It sets boundaries, distances us from harm, and gives us room to breathe again. When we listen to our anger and respond to it with care, we begin to feel protected. Once our nervous systems begin to perceive this safety, other emotions often awaken. Memories surface. Grief, fear, and sadness rise to the top. For some, this might feel overwhelming or confusing, especially if these emotions have been dormant for years. However, in the work of trauma healing, this is often a sign of progress. When safety returns, so does the capacity to feel more fully.

This happened to me not long ago. After asserting strong boundaries in a painful situation, I began to feel something in my body shift. The anger that had protected me gave way to deeper layers of emotion. A younger part of myself, who had carried early childhood pain for years, finally felt safe enough to speak. I cried, reached out for support, journaled, and sat in stillness. Even though it was hard, I knew it was healing and that my anger had protected me long enough for grief to finally find its way to the surface.

If something like this happens for you, please know that it is normal and expected. You are not doing anything wrong. You are simply healing, and your body is telling the story of what you have been through.

This is part of why I often encourage people to build up their support systems before diving into deep anger work. When the layers of emotion begin to surface, it helps to have people you can trust, whether that is a friend, a partner, a community, or a trauma-informed, anti-oppressive therapist. It helps to have people who can say, "I see you. I am here. This matters. You are valid and you are not alone." Healing does not have to happen in isolation. In fact, it rarely does.

With this in mind, anger is not the end of the road. It is an opening that reminds us we are worthy of protection, our stories matter, and our bodies carry wisdom. It reminds us that injustice must be named, and that we have the right to dream of something better. It moves us toward grief and joy, collective action and rest, heartbreak and possibility. It connects us to ancestors who fought for our human rights and to future generations who are counting on us to do the same.

So, let your anger guide you toward truth, showing you where you have been silenced, as well as where your voice is most needed. Let it carve out space for softness and laughter, music and marching, poetry and protest. Let it be the fire that lights the way home.

You are not alone and you never were. There is a great chorus rising with you and within you. As you hold your fire, let this be your reminder that you matter, your voice matters, and your anger may be the very spark that ignites everything beautiful that follows.

Afterword

Find Your Fucking Fire would not exist without the love, support, and encouragement of so many friends, colleagues, and loved ones. In my effort to name people here, I know there is no possible way for me to list every single person. So, if you are in my life and have been part of my journey, consider this your heartfelt thanks. I am grateful for you.

Thank you to Angela Yarber and Tehom Center Publishing for embracing my most impassioned writing ideas. I'm also grateful to the Tehom Author Facebook group for your camaraderie and solidarity.

Trish, thank you for unlocking my lava and fire with singing bowls. Cai, thank you for helping me name what I needed and for opening space to process. Diana, thank you for always sharing the book journey with me, as we both live out our childhood dreams. Patricia and my witchy friends, thank you for offering community as I moved through deep anger and life changes. Kathy, thank you for inviting me onto your podcast where I first said this book's title aloud. Malumir, thank you for being a safe space to give and receive support. You and your fabulous spouse cheered me on the whole way.

Allen, thank you for believing in every one of my wild dreams and encouraging me to chase them. Your support shows up in so many thoughtful ways. Will, River, and Becca, thank you for laughing with me and getting excited about my ideas. You bring delight and energy into my life. Keiko, your quiet cuddles at my feet while I wrote brought comfort and calm. I'm so grateful for you.

To the Instagram and Substack writing communities, thank you for showing up with excitement and encouragement. You remind me that my voice has a place in the world.

Beth Kempton, your outlining method changed my creative life. I've used it for two books now and likely will for every book I write. Your pace inspires me to keep going.

Lama Rod Owens, your books and online presence helped me approach anger through a spiritually grounded, anti-oppressive lens. The reflections and exercises you offer shaped my own journey. I also honor bell hooks' *killing rage*, Soraya Chemaly's *Rage Becomes Her*, and Claudia Rankine's *Citizen*, which each deepened my understanding of anger, identity, and justice.

This book is written for the intersectionally marginalized, including all of us carrying generational trauma while navigating systems never meant for our thriving. May you find validation, clarity, and relief in these pages. I also honor the ancestors, biological and not, who guide us toward justice and remind us that our rage is sacred, our rest is necessary, and our collective power is unstoppable.

Writing this book helped me release years of anger stored in my body. It sparked action, hard conversations, and transformation in my life. My hope is that it offers the same kind of release to others, especially those who are burned out, disillusioned, or navigating injustice, exhaustion, and grief. You are not alone and your fire matters.

About the Author

Anne Kinsey, M.Div., OMC, HMIP (they/them), is an intersectional writer living in rural North Carolina, on the unceded land of the Cheraw and Catawba peoples. They live with their spouse, three children, and a collection of beloved pets. Anne is a trauma-sensitive neurofeedback and HRV biofeedback practitioner, trauma recovery coach, human trafficking consultant, and longtime activist. They are also the founding executive director of Love Powered Life, a nonprofit providing healing services to survivors of human trafficking and their families.

Anne integrates lived experience, somatic practices, and neuroscience-based support in ways that honor the complexity of trauma and identity, always through an intentionally anti-oppressive lens. They hold a Master of Divinity in pastoral care and counseling, alongside extensive continuing education in neurofeedback, HRV biofeedback, trauma-informed care, community organizing, and justice-based consulting. Their work is rooted in deep compassion and a bold commitment to equity and liberation. Anne frequently works with individuals navigating spiritual trauma, deconstruction, or harm experienced in religious settings, creating space for healing that honors personal sovereignty and lived truth.

Anne wrote *Find Your Fucking Fire* while processing long-held anger that had been affecting their body, spirit, and capacity to thrive. What began as a personal toolkit became a book. Their hope is that it now serves others, offering validation, release, and empowerment to anyone navigating burnout, grief, injustice, or the accumulation of unexpressed rage.

Anne is also the author of *Mosaic Hearts: Poems on Being a Queer and Interracial Family in the South*. Through their website, they offer individual coaching, workshops, and consulting for those seeking support for trauma recovery, anti-oppressive practice, and embodied healing.

Connect with Anne at www.annekinsey.com, on Instagram at @anne.kinsey.writes, or on Substack at @annekinsey.